CONSTRUCTION PROJECT MANAGEMENT 101

FOR BEGINNERS & NEW GRADUATES

2024 STUDENT EDITION

P.D. MASON

SUGARDOG PUBLISHING

CONTENTS

INTRODUCTION

Construction Management is an industry that has come a long way since 1997, when I stepped onto my first job site. Back then, it was a world dominated by hard hats, rolls of paper blueprints, manual labor, and advancements in the industry were slow to catch on. It's an arena transformed by technology, innovation, and dynamic leadership strategies. It's more than just bricks and mortar; it's about managing people and resources and efficiently bringing a vision to life. It still is a great profession that shapes our urban landscapes, creates habitats for human life, and powers economic growth.

What is so exciting about construction project management, you might be thinking to yourself. Just look around. The buildings you see, the roads you drive on, the bridges you cross, they're all products of effective construction management. Construction Management is the silent force that brings architectural marvels to life, ensures the safe and timely completion of projects, and silently impacts our lives in ways we often take for granted.

But here's the thing - construction management isn't just about overseeing a project. It is about communication, planning, and problem-solving. It's about juggling budgets, schedules, and quality control. It's about turning a parcel of land into a structure that can withstand the test of time. It's a power, an art, and a science.

And that is why the idea for this book took shape a few years ago.

In "Construction Project Management 101", we will explore the intricacies of this fascinating field. We will journey through its evolution, delve into its importance in today's world, and uncover the true potential of effective construction management. We will explore real-world examples, engage in thought-provoking exercises, and provide specific recommendations to help you navigate your entrance into this often fast-paced and lucrative industry.

So, whether you're a student stepping into the world of Construction Management, an entry-level professional looking to gain new skills, an industry practitioner seeking to stay updated, or simply a DIY enthusiast curious about the field, this book is for you.

In full transparency, I have been a skilled tradesperson since 1997 and have spent nearly all my career in the commercial construction industry. At first, I was a field technician installing my trade in a mix of small commercial projects and residential new construction builds and remodels. As my career progressed, I found I had a knack for the business side of construction. I switched to project management, estimating, and construction management after a decade and a half in the industry.

When I started on the business side of construction, I was as scared to move out of my comfort zone as a deer is when staring down a blazing vehicle barreling down the highway.

Suppose you're new to the construction industry or new to the prospect of construction management. In that case, the one piece of advice I can give you is what I give many new CMs that I meet - and that is to develop a system for yourself that you will remain consistent with throughout your career.

There are many elements of construction management, which equates to many different opportunities for problem-solving, new ideas, and "think outside of the box" moments that become much easier to wade through as you get comfortable and acclimated in a construction management role.

Throughout this book, I will interchangeably reference construction management or manager and project management or manager as they are nearly identical. Later on in this book, we will look at the similarities and differences between the construction manager and the project manager, and you'll understand that although they have different titles, the CM and PM are very similar, with just a few differences between them.

With that, welcome to the world of construction management, and let's turn the page and start building your success!

1

THE FUNDAMENTALS OF CONSTRUCTION PROJECT MANAGEMENT

YOU MAY NOT REALIZE IT, but every time you step into a building, whether it's a towering skyscraper or a cozy condominium, you're stepping into a marvel of construction management. It's an intricate coordination of planning, scheduling, and executing, all aimed at transforming a blueprint into reality.

We start by taking a look into the basics of construction project management. We will explain construction management and why it's crucial in building projects. You'll get a clear picture of what a construction manager does and how their role is central to ensuring a construction project runs smoothly.

Throughout the chapter, we'll walk you through the progressive stages of a construction project, from the initial idea to project turnover. You'll also get to know the construction team, understanding each member's different jobs and responsibilities—architects, engineers, contractors, and more. This chapter will introduce you to the basics of construction project management, equipping you with the essential knowledge for handling construction projects effectively.

DEFINING CONSTRUCTION MANAGEMENT

Construction Management is the heart that pumps life into a construction project. It's the process that bridges the gap between an idea and a tangible structure. It's a discipline that takes a project from concept to completion, managing all the complexities and challenges along the way.

But what exactly does it involve?

Role in Project Development

The role of construction management in project development is similar to a coach's role in a sports game. Just as the coach guides the athletes, ensuring they play in harmony to create a winning strategy, construction management guides a construction project, ensuring all elements work harmoniously to create a successful result.

Construction management involves overseeing the entire project development process. This includes everything from assessing project feasibility to coordinating with stakeholders, from planning the work to ensuring it's executed efficiently. The big-picture perspective ensures the project stays on track, on budget, and on schedule.

Think of a high-rise building project. Before the first brick is laid, construction management is at work. It analyzes the project's feasibility by evaluating factors like site conditions, local regulations, and project cost. It involves selecting the right construction methods, materials, and technology. And it's involved in creating a detailed project plan, outlining the tasks, timelines, and resources needed to complete the job.

Relationship with Clients

Establishing a good relationship with clients in construction management is as important as laying a solid foundation for a building. After all, construction projects are usually significant investments for clients, whether they're homeowners looking to build their dream house or corporations planning a new office complex.

The relationship with clients in construction management is built on trust, communication, and collaboration. As a construction manager, you're not just managing a project; you're managing a client's expectations, concerns, and dreams. You're their advisor, their liaison, and their advocate. You're the one they turn to for updates, for answers, and for assurance.

For instance, if a client wishes to construct an ecologically sustainable home, the construction manager would guide them through the process of selecting eco-friendly materials, integrating energy-efficient systems, and meeting green building standards. The construction manager turns the client's vision into a feasible plan, ensuring the final result aligns with the client's goals, budget, and timeline.

Coordination of Resources

A construction project is a bit like a jigsaw puzzle. There are many pieces - materials, labor, equipment, subcontractors, permits, and so on - and they all must fit together perfectly to complete the picture. This is where a construction manager shines.

Construction management involves coordinating all these resources, ensuring they're available when needed, used efficiently, and managed effectively. It's about ensuring materials are delivered on time, labor is scheduled properly, equipment is maintained, subcontractors are managed, and permits are obtained.

Consider a situation where a construction project is delayed due to the late delivery of materials. This could lead to idle labor, delayed tasks, and increased costs. A construction manager would ensure materials are ordered and delivered on time through effective resource coordination, preventing such delays and associated costs.

Construction management is the glue that holds a construction project together. It's a dynamic, multi-faceted process that requires a deep understanding of the construction industry, a knack for problem-solving, and a solid grasp of project management principles. As we progress through this book, we'll explore each of these aspects in greater detail, equipping you with the knowledge and skills to excel in this exciting field.

THE ROLE OF A CONSTRUCTION MANAGER

A construction manager is the "coach" of sorts in the construction game field. Just like a coach can skillfully coordinate the game playing to bring a team to a win, a construction manager coordinates various elements of a construction project to achieve a successful outcome. This role has many responsibilities, each vital to the project's success.

Overseeing Project Execution

The construction manager is the captain at the helm, steering the ship of project execution. They manage every aspect of the construction process, ensuring tasks are completed on time, within budget, and to the required quality standards.

Picture a construction site bustling with activity. You have laborers pouring concrete, carpenters crafting structures, electricians wiring the building, and many more trades performing their tasks in a race to the completion date. It's a complex balance of activities, and the construction manager is the expert at balancing acts. They manage the schedule, assign tasks, resolve issues, and keep the project moving forward. They are the driving force that propels the project from initiation to completion.

Risk Management

Every construction project comes with its share of risks. It could be unexpected ground conditions, material shortages, weather disruptions, or even regulatory changes. If not managed properly, these risks can derail a project, causing delays, cost overruns, or worse.

This is where the construction manager steps in as the risk manager. They identify potential risks, assess their impact, devise strategies to mitigate them and develop contingency plans. They monitor the project for any signs of these risks materializing and take prompt action when necessary.

For example, imagine a construction project in a region known for its rainy climate. The construction manager, recognizing the risk of weather-related delays, could schedule weather-sensitive activities for the drier months, arrange for protective coverings for the site, and have a contingency plan ready for unforeseen weather events.

Quality Control

Quality is a cornerstone of any construction project. It's what ensures the building stands strong for years, provides a safe and comfortable space for its occupants, and meets the client's expectations. Ensuring this quality is another key responsibility of a construction manager.

The construction manager sets quality standards for the project based on industry norms, regulatory requirements, and client expectations. They implement quality control processes to check the work at every stage, from raw materials to final finishes. They inspect the work, identify any deviations from the standards, and take corrective action.

Consider a scenario where a construction manager notices that the concrete mix used in the foundation does not meet the specified strength requirements. The construction manager would then reject the substandard mix, arrange for a compliant replacement, and ensure the foundation is built with the right quality of concrete.

Communication with Stakeholders

A construction project is a collaborative endeavor. It involves many stakeholders - clients, designers, contractors, subcontractors, suppliers, regulatory authorities, etc. Managing their expectations, resolving their concerns, and ensuring their cooperation are essential for the project's success. This is achieved through effective communication, another critical role of a construction manager.

The construction manager acts as the central communication hub of the project. They keep all stakeholders informed about the project's progress, discuss any issues or changes with them, and ensure their input is considered in decision-making. They hold regular meetings, send out updates, and are always available to answer questions or address concerns.

Imagine a situation where a design change is proposed mid-project, which could impact the project's cost and timeline. In such a scenario, the construction manager would discuss the change with all affected stakeholders, explain its implications, explore alternatives, and facilitate a decision that balances the project's objectives and the stakeholders' interests.

As you see, the role of a construction manager is multifaceted and demanding. It requires a broad skill set, a deep understanding of the construction process, and an ability to juggle multiple responsibilities. However, it is also immensely rewarding, as it allows you to shape the built environment and make a lasting impact on the community.

KEY STAGES IN THE CONSTRUCTION PROCESS

Just as a well-rehearsed playbook has movements that follow a logical progression, a construction project adheres to a structure that takes it from concept to completion. This structure can be broken down into five key stages, each integral to the project's overall success.

Project Initiation

The first phase of a construction project is similar to the initial encounter between a sports recruiter and prospective athletes. It's the moment when the game plan is outlined, player roles are assigned, and the atmosphere for the impending game is established. In construction project lingo, this corresponds to the kickoff stage, where the project's viability is evaluated, and the foundation for the entire endeavor is established.

During project initiation, the key players come together to discuss the project's objectives, requirements, and constraints. This is where the project's feasibility is evaluated, considering factors like budget, timeline, and regulatory requirements. A feasibility report is drafted, which serves as an initial checklist outlining the project's viability and potential challenges.

Planning and Design

Next, we transition to the strategizing and playbook development stage, similar to the rigorous practice sessions leading up to a sports team's big game. This is where the project's finer details are fine-tuned, and an all-encompassing game plan is crafted.

The planning phase involves a detailed breakdown of the project's tasks, assigning responsibilities, and setting the project timeline. A project plan is developed, which outlines the project's scope, schedule, cost, and quality targets. This plan serves as the road map for the project, guiding the team through each step of the process.

Simultaneously, the design phase gets underway. Architects and engineers collaborate to transform the client's vision into a practical design. This design is then translated into detailed blueprints, which serve as a guide for the construction team.

Execution and Construction

With the game plan and strategy locked in, it's now the moment for the teams to unite - the execution and construction phase. This mirrors a live sports match, where each athlete plays their role to forge a seamless team performance. This is the phase where the tough, physical work takes center stage in the construction project.

During the execution and construction stage, the blueprints are brought to life. The construction team swings into action, building the structure as per the design specifications. Each task is executed according to the project plan, with resources managed and coordinated efficiently to ensure smooth progress.

Monitoring and Control

In a sports match, the coach keeps a vigilant eye on the players, ensuring that the game follows the planned strategies and tactics. Similarly, a construction project's monitoring and control phase involves overseeing its advancement closely, ensuring it remains on course.

During this stage, the construction manager monitors the project's progress against the project plan. Any deviations from the plan, be it cost overruns, schedule delays, or quality issues, are promptly identified and addressed. Regular reports are generated to inform all stakeholders about the project's status.

Project Closure

Finally, we reach the project's closeout stage, much like the concluding moments of a sports match when the athletes acknowledge the crowd. This is the phase where the project is officially wrapped up, and the ultimate result is handed over to the client.

The project closure stage involves a final inspection of the completed structure, checking for any defects or issues. Once any necessary corrections are made, the completed project is handed over to the client. This stage also includes a project review, where the team reflects on the project's successes and challenges, gleaning valuable insights for future projects.

By following this structured approach, a construction project can be managed effectively from start to finish. Each stage is interconnected, with the success of one stage influencing the others. The goal is to ensure that the final product, much like a well-played game, is a testament to the harmonious coordination of various elements, reflecting the dedication, skill, and effort of all involved. A well-managed construction project is an art form of concrete, steel, and glass - a testament to human ingenuity and the power of effective management.

THE CONSTRUCTION TEAM: ROLES AND RESPONSIBILITIES

A construction project oftentimes mirrors a finely-tuned sports team, where every athlete plays a distinct yet interconnected role. In the construction world, these athletes are replaced by a diverse team of professionals, each contributing their unique skills and expertise to the game plan.

Project Manager

At the helm of this team is the Project Manager. However, an intricate project plan replaces the Project Managers' playbook. Project Managers ensure the project runs smoothly, stays within budget, and is completed on time.

They oversee all aspects of the project, from the initial planning to the final project turnover. Their role includes setting objectives, defining the scope, developing schedules, and managing resources. They are the central point of communication between all stakeholders, including clients, contractors, suppliers, and regulatory bodies.

For instance, think of a scenario where a project is running behind schedule. The Project Manager would analyze the situation, identify the cause of the delay, and devise a strategy to get the project back on track, coordinating with all relevant parties to implement the plan.

Site Engineer

Next in line is the Site Engineer, a role similar to a sports team general manager. They play a leading role in the actual construction process, translating the technical designs into physical structures. Site Engineers oversee the day-to-day operations on the construction site, ensuring that work is carried out as per the project plan and design specifications.

Their duties encompass a range of activities, from supervising construction workers to inspecting materials, from solving on-site technical issues to ensuring adherence to safety standards.

If there is ever a situation where the construction team encounters an unexpected sub-surface condition, like an underground utility line not marked on the site plan, the Site Engineer would assess the situation, liaise with the utility company, and adjust the construction plan to avoid the utility line, ensuring work continues safely and efficiently.

Quantity Surveyor

A Quantity Surveyor's main role is carefully managing the project's budget and contracts. Quantity Surveyors navigate the financial landscape of a construction project, ensuring it stays on par in terms of cost-effectiveness without compromising quality.

Their role involves estimating and controlling project costs, preparing contracts, valuing completed work, and managing design or work schedule changes that may impact costs.

Imagine a situation where a client requests a design change that involves using a more expensive material than initially planned. The Quantity Surveyor would calculate the additional cost, assess its impact on the overall project budget, and advise the client and the Project Manager on the best course of action.

Health and Safety Officer

Last but not least, the construction site is the Health and Safety Officer. The Health and Safety Officer protects the construction site, ensuring it's a secure and hazard-free zone for all team members.

They are responsible for implementing and monitoring safety policies, conducting regular safety inspections, and ensuring compliance with occupational health and safety regulations.

For example, if a construction worker were to suffer an injury on-site, the Health and Safety Officer would investigate the incident, identify any safety lapses, and take corrective measures to prevent similar incidents in the future.

Just as a championship-winning sports team relies on the skills and commitment of its players, the success of a construction project hinges on its dedicated team. Each team member fulfills a pivotal role, expertise, and unwavering dedication to molding the project's final result. This united effort turns a mere concept into a constructed building, an idea into a concrete structure, and a vision into a tangible reality. As we move forward, we will explore these roles in greater detail, providing you with a deeper insight into the dynamics at work within a construction project.

As we conclude this chapter, let's take a moment to appreciate the collection of skills, efforts, and coordination that go into every construction project. This coordinated effort paves the way for the structures around us, crafts our skylines, and shapes our built environment. And it's this coordination that you, as a part of the construction world, contribute to.

2

EXPLORING THE SECTORS IN CONSTRUCTION MANAGEMENT

LIFE IS A FINELY CRAFTED structure woven with the interlacing threads of diverse experiences and perspectives. Each thread and experience contributes a unique color and texture, forming a vibrant reflection of life's diversity. In the construction management domain, every sector —residential, commercial, industrial, and infrastructure—serves as a distinct strand, adding its own hue to the tapestry of the construction industry.

RESIDENTIAL CONSTRUCTION MANAGEMENT

Residential construction is the art of crafting homes and spaces that offer comfort, security, and a sense of belonging. As a residential construction manager, you are privileged to sculpt these spaces, shaping environments where families grow, friendships flourish, and life unfolds.

Single-Family Homes

Building a single-family home is like bringing a family's dream to life. Each project is a unique expression, reflecting the homeowner's individual tastes and lifestyle. Whether it's a cozy suburban bungalow or a grand mansion with a panoramic view, your role involves understanding the client's vision, planning for space and functionality, and ensuring a blend of quality and aesthetics.

Multi-Family Buildings

Multi-family buildings, such as apartments and duplexes, present a different facet of residential construction. These larger-scale projects demand higher levels of coordination involving complex building systems. As a construction manager, you navigate the challenges of high-density construction, balancing the needs of multiple residents and adhering to building codes. The goal is to create a sense of community and provide amenities that enhance residents' quality of life.

Renovations and Remodels

Renovations and remodels add another layer to the residential construction spectrum. Projects like kitchen remodels or room additions require a unique set of skills. As a construction manager, you must work within the existing structure's constraints, seamlessly blending old and new elements while minimizing disruption to occupants.

Every facet of residential construction offers unique challenges and rewards, each contributing to the shared goal of creating spaces people are proud to call home.

COMMERCIAL CONSTRUCTION MANAGEMENT

Beneath the towering skyscrapers, in the midst of bustling city streets, lies the dynamic world of commercial construction management. This is where business shapes the concrete and steel defining our urban landscapes.

Office Buildings

Office buildings are the economic pulse of a city, housing minds that drive progress and collaboration. As a commercial construction manager, you craft these hubs of productivity. Each project presents a unique challenge—balancing functionality with aesthetics, creating flexible spaces, and integrating advanced technological systems.

Retail Centers

Retail centers are vibrant marketplaces where commerce comes alive. Constructing these spaces from shopping malls to boutique stores requires understanding consumer behavior and store layout strategies. As a construction manager, you create inviting spaces that facilitate traffic flow and deliver a memorable shopping experience.

Hotels and Restaurants

Hotels and restaurants serve as havens for relaxation, dining, and celebration. As a construction manager in this sector, you create welcoming spaces catering to diverse needs. Projects involve adhering to strict health and safety regulations, creating functional and visually appealing spaces, and constructing buildings that embody the spirit of hospitality.

Each domain—office buildings, retail centers, hotels, and restaurants—offers a unique flavor to the exciting world of commercial construction management. While they require different skills and cater to distinct demands, they all contribute to the shared objective of driving commerce, fueling growth, and shaping the city's commercial landscape.

INDUSTRIAL CONSTRUCTION MANAGEMENT

This domain is a robust anchor in the industrial construction management sector, providing profound depth and unwavering strength. It's where efficiency converges with expansiveness, precision merges with resilience, and industry mechanics seamlessly mesh with the rising pace of progress.

Factories and Manufacturing Plants

Factories and manufacturing plants are the dynamic hubs of our industrial landscape, where raw materials transform into products. As an industrial construction manager, your role is to coordinate these transformations. Building a factory involves meticulous planning for efficient workflow, installing specialized machinery, and adhering to strict safety and environmental standards.

Warehouses and Storage Facilities

Warehouses and storage facilities are the silent custodians of the industrial sector, vital links in the supply chain network. Constructing these spaces involves optimizing space, facilitating accessibility, and ensuring safe and efficient storage. Imagine constructing a distribution center for a large e-commerce company, requiring detailed planning, logistical expertise, and a focus on efficiency and speed.

Power Plants

Power plants are the heartbeats of the industrial sector, providing energy for cities and industries. Constructing a power plant involves implementing intricate technical plans, managing large-scale civil works, installing heavy machinery, and adhering to stringent safety and environmental regulations. Consider the construction of a nuclear power plant, a project requiring a blend of engineering expertise and project management professionalism.

Industrial projects are challenging but highly rewarding in the grand scheme of construction management. They're about creating infrastructures that power our industries, support our economies, and drive our progress.

INFRASTRUCTURE AND PUBLIC WORKS CONSTRUCTION MANAGEMENT

Look around, and you'll see roads guiding us, bridges connecting landscapes, and utilities making modern life possible. This is the realm of infrastructure and public works construction management—a world that silently but profoundly impacts our daily lives.

Roads and Highways

Roads and highways are the lifelines of our communities, facilitating movement and fostering connections. Constructing them involves a complex dance of planning, coordination, and execution, considering factors like traffic volume, safety standards, and environmental impact.

Bridges and Tunnels

Bridges and tunnels are engineering marvels overcoming natural barriers. Building them requires a deep understanding of engineering principles, meticulous planning, and precise execution. Envision constructing a suspension bridge, coordinating with marine and environmental authorities to ensure safe construction.

Public Utilities

Public utilities—water supply, sewage systems, electrical grids—are the invisible backbone of our cities. Constructing and maintaining them involves tasks from laying pipelines to upgrading sewage treatment plants. Think about the responsibility of constructing a water treatment plant, ensuring safe and efficient water treatment.

Each element—roads and highways, bridges and tunnels, public utilities—forms a critical piece of the infrastructure puzzle. They're enablers of progress, facilitators of connectivity, and sustainers of modern life. As you step into the world of infrastructure and public works construction management, remember the profound impact of your work. You're not just constructing structures; you're building the foundations of society, one project at a time.

As we turn the page on this chapter, reflect on the diverse landscapes of construction management we've traversed. From the warmth of residential construction to the pulse of commercial projects, from the strength of industrial setups to the vital infrastructure veins. Each sector enriches our perspective, deepening our appreciation of this fascinating field. Moving forward, let's carry these insights as our baseline to navigate the construction terrain that lies ahead.

3

THE INNER WORKINGS OF A BUILDING

IMAGINE WALKING through a bustling construction site, the air filled with the hum of machinery and the distinct rhythm of progress. Steel beams reach skyward, concrete forms take shape, and intricate networks of pipes and wires begin their crisscross intersections. As a construction manager, it's your responsibility to understand and coordinate this jigsaw puzzle of building systems and materials. This chapter will lay the groundwork for that understanding, offering a solid foundation in building science that you can build upon in your construction management career.

UNDERSTANDING BUILDING SYSTEMS AND MATERIALS

Much like the human body, a building is a complex system of interrelated parts, each serving a specific function, yet all working harmoniously to support the structure's overall performance. Let's look at these systems and the materials that bring them to life.

Structural Systems

The structural system is the skeleton of a building, providing the framework that supports and distributes the structure's load. It includes elements such as beams, columns, slabs, and foundations. Different materials can be used in structural systems with unique properties and applications.

- **Steel**: Known for its strength and durability, steel is commonly used in constructing skyscrapers and large commercial buildings. It's also used in residential construction for elements like steel framing and reinforcement bars in concrete.
- **Concrete**: Concrete is versatile, durable, and has excellent compression strength, making it suitable for foundations and load-bearing walls. It is often reinforced with steel bars (rebar) to enhance its tensile strength.
- **Wood**: Wood is lightweight, easy to work with, and provides sound insulation. It's widely used in residential construction for framing, flooring, and roofing.

Mechanical Systems

Mechanical systems in a building include heating, ventilation, and air conditioning (HVAC) systems. These systems control the indoor climate, ensuring comfortable living conditions and good air quality.

- **Heating and Cooling Units**: These devices control the temperature in a building. They can range from furnaces and boilers to air conditioners and heat pumps.
- **Ductwork**: Ducts are the channels that distribute heated or cooled air throughout the building. They are typically made of sheet metal, fiberglass, or flexible plastic.
- **Ventilation Systems**: These systems exchange indoor air with fresh outdoor air, controlling humidity levels and removing pollutants.

Electrical Systems

Electrical systems power the lights, appliances, and devices in a building. They include components like wiring, outlets, switches, and circuit breakers.

- **Wiring**: Electrical wires carry power from the service panel to outlets and fixtures. They are usually made of copper or aluminum and are insulated with a plastic coating.
- **Outlets and Switches**: Outlets provide access points for plugging in appliances and devices. Switches control the flow of electricity to lights and other fixtures.
- **Circuit Breakers:** Located in the service panel, circuit breakers protect the electrical circuits by interrupting the flow of electricity when a fault is detected.

Plumbing Systems

Plumbing systems provide a building with clean water and dispose of wastewater. They include pipes, fixtures, and drains.

- **Pipes**: Pipes carry water to and from a building. They can be made of various materials, including copper, PVC (polyvinyl chloride), and PEX (cross-linked polyethylene).
- **Fixtures**: Fixtures like faucets, showers, and toilets control water flow. They are typically made of stainless steel, brass, or plastic.
- **Drains**: Drains remove wastewater from a building and direct it to the sewer or septic system. They are usually made of ABS (acrylonitrile butadiene styrene) or PVC.

Understanding these building systems and materials is like learning the alphabet. It equips you with the basic knowledge you need to understand the complexity of your construction project. It enables you to make informed decisions, manage your resources effectively, and ensure the quality and performance of your building. As we proceed, we'll dive deeper into these topics, providing a knowledge base to build your skills and enrich your construction management confidence.

THE ROLE OF DESIGN IN CONSTRUCTION

Preconstruction design is the first task in the typical sequence of building a structure. It sets the stage, dictates the schedule, and directs all the following work. The construction design process involves various specializations, each contributing to the final product. These include architectural design, structural design, and mechanical, electrical, and plumbing (MEP) systems design.

Architectural Design

Think of architectural design as the beginning of the pre-construction process. It all starts with an idea, a concept, a vision. Architects take this vision and translate it into a tangible design. They consider the client's needs, the site's characteristics, the project's context, and many other factors to create an aesthetically pleasing and functionally efficient design.

Architectural design is not just about creating appealing and sustainable buildings; it's about creating spaces people can use and enjoy. It's about designing a smooth layout, choosing materials that enhance the building's character, and incorporating details that reflect the client's personality.

For instance, consider the process of designing a hospital. The architect must consider patient comfort, staff efficiency, and medical equipment requirements. They would create a layout that facilitates easy movement, select durable and easy-to-clean materials, and incorporate details like adequate lighting and noise control.

Structural Design

If architectural design is the first thing that happens in construction, structural design isn't far behind. Structural engineers take the architectural design and ensure it can stand up in the real world. They calculate the loads the building will have to support, determine the stresses the materials will face, and design the structural elements to withstand these forces.

Structural design aims to ensure that a building is safe and stable. It's about choosing suitable materials, determining the correct sizes for beams and columns, and designing the foundations to support the structure.

Imagine the process of designing a high-rise building. The structural engineer would need to calculate the loads from the building's weight, the occupants, and environmental factors like wind and earthquakes. They then design the building's structural system to resist these loads, selecting materials and dimensions that offer the required strength and stability.

Mechanical, Electrical, and Plumbing (MEP) Design

In the pre-construction process, MEP design is often concurrently with the structural design. MEP engineers design the mechanical, electrical, and plumbing systems that make a building comfortable, functional, and safe.

Mechanical design involves the heating, ventilation, and air conditioning (HVAC) systems that control the building's climate. Electrical design includes the wiring, outlets, and systems that power the building's lights and appliances. Plumbing design covers the pipes, fixtures, and systems that provide water and remove waste.

Picture the process of designing the MEP systems for a large office building. The engineers would need to design an HVAC system that can maintain a comfortable temperature across multiple floors, an electrical system that can support a variety of office equipment and a plumbing system that can provide adequate water supply and drainage for the building's occupants.

As you can see, the role of design in pre-construction is multifaceted and critical. It is the starting point of the construction process, setting the trajectory for the entire project. It requires creativity, technical knowledge, and a deep understanding of the building's purpose and context. As a construction manager, understanding design aspects can help you better coordinate with the design team, manage construction activities more effectively, and deliver a building that meets the client's expectations and the project's objectives.

KEY PRINCIPLES OF STRUCTURAL ENGINEERING

Load-Bearing Structures

In nearly every building, load-bearing components provide the backbone and the framework that keeps the tallest skyscrapers upright and the smallest residential homes intact in a heavy storm. Load-bearing components are the stalwart pillars and walls that shoulder the weight of the building, supporting and transferring the load to the foundation and eventually, the earth.

Load-bearing structures aren't just about brute strength but a delicate balance of forces. Load-bearing components can be walls, columns, or slabs made from various materials such as concrete, steel, or wood. The key to their success lies in their ability to withstand compression forces (which compress or compact the material) and tensile forces (which stretch or pull apart the material).

They need to stand tall against the weight of the building, the pressure of the wind, the shaking of an earthquake, and the dynamic loads of occupants and furniture.

Take a concrete wall, for example. It's not just a partition; it plays a vital role in supporting the floors above, resisting the earth's pressure on a basement wall, or carrying the roof load in a single-story building. Understanding these structural roles and responsibilities is crucial for effective construction management.

As we continue into construction management, these foundational principles will serve as our roadmap, helping us comprehend the intricate interplay of forces and materials that make up the complete building.

Material Strength and Properties

Every structure built has its unique design and characteristics, and every material in a building has its exceptional strength and properties. The choice of material for a system is a critical decision that influences the building's durability, safety, and even aesthetics.

As we touched on briefly at the beginning of this chapter, materials such as steel, concrete, and wood each bring unique strengths to a building. With its high strength-to-weight ratio and flexibility, steel is ideal for resisting tensile forces. Concrete, on the other hand, excels at withstanding compressive forces. Wood, while not as strong as steel or concrete, is lighter and easier to work with, making it a popular choice for residential construction.

But it's not just about strength; other properties of materials also play a crucial role. Thermal conductivity affects a building's insulation, acoustic properties impact sound transmission, and resistance to fire can be a lifesaver in case of a fire. Therefore, every material needs to be chosen carefully, considering its strengths, weaknesses, and the project's specific demands.

For instance, consider the choice of material for a bridge. With its high strength and flexibility, steel might be an excellent choice for the bridge deck. However, for the piers, which are subjected to high compressive forces, concrete might be a better fit.

Structural Analysis

In the design of a building, structural analysis is critical. Although many designers or structural engineers have given their stamp of approval for the plan, structural analysis is a process that examines a structure's response to loads, helping to predict how the building will behave under various conditions.

Structural analysis involves a series of calculations and simulations. It begins with identifying the loads that the structure will be subjected to, such as dead loads (the weight of the building itself), live loads (occupants, furniture, etc.), and environmental loads (wind, snow, etc.).

Next, the analysis calculates the internal forces these loads generate within the structure, such as tension, compression, and shear. The structural elements are then checked to ensure they have adequate strength and stiffness to resist these forces without failing or deforming excessively.

Imagine you're analyzing a multi-story office building. You would calculate the loads from the building's weight, the occupants, the furniture, and wind pressure. You would then determine the forces these loads would generate in the building's beams, columns, and slabs. Then, checking against the strength and stiffness of these elements would ensure that the building is safe and serviceable.

Mastering structural engineering principles is akin to learning the language of buildings. It allows you to understand their dialogues of forces and materials, predict their behavior under different conditions, and design safe, efficient, and durable structures. As you continue your exploration of construction management, this understanding will be your trusted guide, helping you make informed decisions, solve complex problems, and deliver successful projects.

SAFETY STANDARDS AND BUILDING CODES

Let's discuss safety in construction and how protection is vital for a successful construction project. In the world of construction, there are rules that everyone follows to ensure that the final result isn't just impressive but is also safe, accessible, and fits well with its surroundings.

Occupational Safety and Health Administration (OSHA) Standards

Construction sites are filled with potential hazards, from loud machinery to the risk of falling objects. OSHA is like the safety watchdog throughout the US, setting strict standards to keep everyone safe and able to return to their families on the construction site at the end of the day.

OSHA standards are like the rulebook within any sports event; OSHA's rule book, however, only applies in construction. They guide workers, ensuring every step is taken with safety in mind. These standards require using personal protective equipment, providing safe procedures for equipment operation, and laying out measures to prevent falls, electrocutions, and other common site hazards.

Let's say workers are putting up a steel frame. OSHA standards say, "Strap on those safety harnesses to prevent falls, put on hard hats to shield against falling objects, and wear safety glasses to protect from flying debris." They would also detail safe ways to operate cranes and handle steel beams, turning what could be a risky task into a carefully coordinated safety routine.

International Building Code (IBC)

The International Building Code (IBC) is the blueprint for constructing a building. It lays out the guidelines, the specifications, and the procedures for building construction. This code presents a comprehensive set of rules that address construction's structural, fire, and life safety aspects, ensuring that buildings are secure, resilient, and suitable for occupancy.

The IBC covers a broad spectrum of topics, ranging from fundamental principles of structural design to fire resistance ratings and from plumbing and mechanical systems to measures for energy conservation. Updated every three years, it incorporates technological advancements, materials, and construction methods, keeping the industry aligned with the latest trends.

For example, in the design of a high-rise building, the IBC would outline the minimum requirements for strength and stability, fire resistance ratings for various components, and specifications for emergency exits and fire suppression systems. This ensures that the building is well-equipped to withstand natural forces and emergencies.

Americans with Disabilities Act (ADA) Standards

In the blueprint of construction, ADA standards are crucial in ensuring that every participant in the experience is included and catered to. These standards outline how buildings should be planned and constructed to be accessible to individuals with disabilities, ensuring everyone can fully engage in the experience.

ADA standards address various design elements, covering parking, pathways, entrances, exits, restrooms, elevators, signage, and emergency systems. Their goal is to guarantee that individuals with disabilities can independently, safely, and comfortably navigate and utilize the building.

Take, for instance, the planning of a public library. ADA standards would guide the design of accessible parking spaces, ramps, and pathways. They would set specifications for counter heights, restroom layouts, and the arrangement of bookshelves. The aim is to ensure that the library isn't just a repository of knowledge but a welcoming space accessible to all community members.

Local Zoning Laws and Regulations

In construction, local zoning laws and regulations act as the guiding instructions. They define the rules for what can be constructed where, directing the placement, size, and purpose of buildings. These regulations ensure that the construction performance aligns harmoniously with its surroundings, contributing positively to the community and the environment.

Zoning laws differ across localities but generally oversee land use, building height, density, parking, and green spaces. They shape the growth of neighborhoods, commercial districts, industrial zones, and other areas, promoting a balanced and sustainable development.

Let's say you're considering building a shopping mall. Local zoning laws would specify the allowable location, height restrictions, required parking spaces, and the amount of green space to be maintained. They aim to ensure the mall is a suitable addition to the community, meeting its needs without disrupting its established character.

Safety standards and building codes are essential in the intricate process of building. They serve as guidelines that shape our actions, ensuring our facilities are safe, accessible, and environmentally friendly. Think of them as the directors overseeing the construction process, guiding us toward an impressive, responsible, sustainable, and harmonious performance with the community and the environment. As we navigate the dynamic world of construction management, these standards and codes become our compass, influencing our decisions, shaping our actions, and leading us toward success. Let's embrace these guidelines, follow these rules, and create buildings that aren't just structures but symbols of safety, inclusivity, and sustainability.

As we conclude this chapter, remember that the science of building isn't just about materials and forces; it's about people, communities, and the environment. It's about crafting safe, functional, and harmonious structures with their surroundings. Envision construction sites as spaces where the building process unfolds, where every element resonates with the principles of safety, accessibility, and sustainability. Moving forward, we'll explore how we can manage this process and ensure the final result is a building that serves as a testament to the science, the art, and the heart of construction.

4

PROJECT PLANNING AND CONTROL TECHNIQUES

THIS CHAPTER EXPLORES the construction management fundamentals, centering around the Critical Path Method (CPM). Uncover the practical application of CPM—a tool that brings order to complexity. From identifying critical paths to streamlining project timelines, enhance your understanding of mastering strategic planning and effective control. This chapter lays the groundwork for successful construction tasks, offering insights that make project management a disciplined and organized process for optimal efficiency. You are designing a construction site where every task aligns purposefully, shaping progress in construction management.

Our initial step in this systematic approach is the Critical Path Method, a valuable project management tool that assists us in mapping out the trajectory of our construction project. It enables us to pinpoint the most vital tasks, estimate their durations, arrange them logically, and calculate the critical path—the series of tasks that dictates the project's duration.

CRITICAL PATH METHOD IN CONSTRUCTION

Let's explore the Critical Path Method in construction. The CPM serves as our roadmap, much like a navigation system installed in many passenger vehicles on the road. It directs us through our project's various tasks, allowing us to navigate our construction path effectively.

Identifying Critical Tasks

Having a good understanding of the duties involved in project management, our construction project involves many tasks—think of them as individual steps in a process. Specific tasks carry more weight, similar to the importance of particular actions in a process. These are critical tasks because they directly impact the project's timeline. Any delay in these tasks would cause a delay in the overall project.

Consider, for instance, the task of laying the foundation of a building. Until the foundation is complete, erecting walls or installing the roof is impossible. Therefore, it's identified as a critical task, and timely completion is vital for the project's advancement.

Estimating Duration for Each Task

Once we've pinpointed our critical tasks, the subsequent step involves estimating the time required for each task. This process is comparable to determining the duration of each step in our project.

To estimate task duration, various factors come into play. These factors include the scope of the task, the availability of resources, and potential delays or disruptions.

For instance, in estimating the time needed to complete the foundation, we would assess the size and complexity of the foundation, the available workforce, the equipment at our disposal, and the potential impact of weather conditions.

. . .

Sequencing Tasks

With our tasks identified and their durations estimated, we need to determine how they should be performed. This is like arranging the pieces on a chess board where our project's correct placement of tasks (chess pieces) ensures smooth and efficient execution.

In construction, tasks often have dependencies—they rely on other tasks to be completed before starting. For instance, we can't start painting the walls until the drywall is installed. So, the task of painting is dependent on the task of drywall installation.

Calculating the Critical Path

Here's where the magic happens. Once we have our tasks sequenced, we can calculate the critical path—the longest sequence of tasks in the project. This path determines the shortest time in which the project can be completed. Any delay in tasks on this path will result in a delay in the project's completion.

Imagine you're planning a relay race, and your team is your project. Each runner (task) needs to complete their leg (duration) in a specific order (sequence) for your team to win (complete the project on time). The critical path is the runner you're most concerned about—the one whose performance will ultimately decide the race's outcome—the project.

In our construction process, the CPM serves as a guiding force. It directs us through the sequence of tasks, ensuring we navigate from one step to the next, and then the next, and so on. With each step completed, we are hitting each milestone at the appropriate time. It plays a crucial role in helping us achieve a construction project that is timely, within budget, and well-executed. As we further examine construction management, the CPM method remains our checklist of sorts, aiding us in coordinating projects with precision, efficiency, and success.

GANTT CHARTS AND THEIR APPLICATIONS

A Gantt chart acts as a visual representation of a construction project, illustrating the sequence of tasks and their coordination. It's a tool that visually outlines the project's timeline, specifying when each task begins, its duration, and how tasks are interconnected. Let's explore utilizing this tool for effective project planning and control.

Listing Tasks

To create a Gantt chart, the initial step is to compile a list of all the tasks involved in the project. Think of it as jotting down the steps in our construction plan. Each item on the list represents a task that needs completion.

For instance, in a home construction project, tasks may include obtaining permits, site preparation, foundation laying, structure framing, and utility installation. Tasks are arranged in the order they must be accomplished, forming a clear roadmap of the project's progression.

Setting Time Frames

Once we have our tasks listed, we determine the duration for each task. This is similar to defining the time each step in our plan should take.

We estimate the duration based on the task's scope, available resources, and dependencies between tasks. For example, laying the foundation might take two weeks, while framing the structure might require three weeks.

These durations are then marked on a timeline, where each task is represented as a horizontal bar spanning its specific duration. The outcome visually represents the project schedule, indicating when each task should commence and conclude.

. . .

Tracking Progress

As the project advances, the Gantt chart acts as a tool for tracking progress, aiding us in monitoring the flow of our construction plan. We can modify the chart to mirror the real-time advancement of tasks, offering an up-to-date snapshot of the project's status.

For instance, if laying the foundation is finished a few days ahead of schedule, we can modify the corresponding section on the Gantt chart accordingly. This enables us to quickly gauge the project's advancement, pinpoint any deviations from the plan, and implement corrective measures if needed.

Visualizing Overlaps and Dependencies

A key advantage of a Gantt chart lies in its capacity to illustrate task dependencies and overlaps, similar to grasping the interconnectedness of elements in a cohesive structure. It enables us to observe how different tasks converge to shape the overall project.

In a Gantt chart, tasks reliant on one another are connected with arrows, indicating their sequence. If a task hinges on the completion of another, the chart denotes this interdependence.

Similarly, if specific tasks can be executed simultaneously, the Gantt chart displays them as overlapping bars. This feature aids in optimizing the project schedule, allowing the arrangement of overlapping duties to make the most efficient use of resources and time.

In the comprehensive execution of a construction project, the Gantt chart emerges as a valuable tool. It aids in crafting our project plan, overseeing project execution, and refining our performance. This tool provides clarity amidst the intricacies of project management, facilitating the coordination of tasks, effective time management, and the successful delivery of the project. It's more than just a chart; it is the visual "taskmaster" of sorts to ensure that the critical path methodology has little to no disruption.

So, as we continue to navigate the dynamic realm of construction management, let's leverage the capabilities of the Gantt chart to create construction projects that are not only well-coordinated but also aesthetically pleasing.

RESOURCE LEVELLING AND ALLOCATION

Building a structure is like assembling a small piece of DIY furniture, with each piece representing a resource necessary to complete the picture. In construction management, these pieces manifest as labor, materials, equipment, time, and money. Managing these resources effectively is similar to playing a strategic game of chess, where the goal is to utilize each piece to its fullest potential while maintaining a balance on the board. Let's explore the moves involved in this strategic game, known as resource leveling and allocation.

Identifying Resource Requirements

Your first move in this game is to take stock of your pieces— identifying the resources required for your construction project. This is a critical step, as it forms the basis of your resource management strategy.

Think about building a house. You need labor to perform various tasks, materials to construct the structure, equipment to facilitate the work, and time and money to enable it all. Determining these requirements involves a detailed analysis of the project plan, considering the scope of work, the sequence of tasks, the project timeline, and the budget.

Your analysis should be thorough and realistic, considering all possible factors affecting the resource requirements. For instance, labor requirements may vary depending on the complexity of tasks, material quantities can change based on design specifications, and equipment needs can fluctuate with the project's progress.

. . .

Balancing Resource Demand and Supply

Once you've identified your resource requirements, the next move is to balance the demand and supply of resources. This involves matching the resources needed to complete the project with the resources available.

Consider a project requiring ten stone masons to lay bricks for a wall. If you only have six masons available, you have a resource imbalance. You'll need to adjust the project schedule, bring in additional masons, or find other ways to close the gap.

Balancing resource demand and supply is a dynamic process. It requires constant monitoring and adjustment as the project progresses, ensuring that resources are always available when needed. It's a delicate dance requiring precision, agility, and foresight.

Optimizing Resource Use

After balancing the demand and supply, your next move is to optimize the use of resources. This is about maximizing efficiency, ensuring that each resource is used to its fullest potential without waste.

Optimization strategies can vary based on the type of resource. For labor, it could mean scheduling workers in shifts to keep the site operational throughout the day. For materials, it could involve ordering in bulk to take advantage of discounts or using prefabricated components to reduce waste. For equipment, it could mean coordinating tasks to minimize idle time.

Remember, optimization is not just about cutting costs—it's about enhancing value. It's about balancing resource use and project outcomes, ensuring every resource contributes to the project's success.

Resolving Resource Conflicts

In the game of resource management, conflicts are inevitable. They arise when resources are scarce, schedules overlap, or unforeseen circumstances disrupt the project plan. Your final move in this game is to resolve these conflicts, ensuring your project stays on track despite the challenges.

Resolving resource conflicts requires problem-solving skills, negotiation tactics, and contingency planning. If you're short on labor, you might need to reschedule tasks, bring in temporary workers, or even automate specific processes. If materials are delayed, you might need to source from a different supplier, substitute with available materials, or adjust the construction sequence to work around the delay.

Resource leveling and allocation play a crucial role in the comprehensive construction management strategy. It's a strategic game, much like chess, where your construction site serves as the board, resources act as the pieces, and the ultimate goal is a successful project. By mastering this strategic approach, you can ensure that your construction site operates in perfect coordination. Each resource fulfills its role at the right time, contributing to a performance that is efficient, cost-effective, and aligned with your project objectives.

TIME-COST TRADEOFF ANALYSIS

In construction management, time and cost are like the intricate interplay of elements in a complex structure. They are interconnected, influencing each other and shaping the overall performance of a project. Managing this time-cost relationship is similar to orchestrating a well-coordinated system, striking the right balance between elements to create a cohesive whole. Let's refine our understanding of this crucial aspect of construction management, examining the nuances of time-cost tradeoff analysis.

Understanding the Time-Cost Relationship

The construction site serves as a platform where the interaction of time and cost takes center stage. Every action and every element in this dynamic interplay affects the project's timeline and budget.

Grasping this relationship between time and cost is essential for effectively managing your construction project.

Time and cost in construction share a mutual relationship. The price tends to rise when we speed up the project by employing more resources or working extra hours. Conversely, the project's duration increases when we extend the timeline to save on costs.

Imagine you're constructing a residential building, and the client wants it completed a month earlier than planned. To meet this new deadline, you might have to bring in additional workers, work double shifts, or expedite material deliveries, which would increase the project cost.

Analyzing Trade-Off Scenarios

With an understanding of the time-cost relationship, we can now analyze tradeoff scenarios. This involves examining various options where adjusting the time could increase or decrease the cost and vice versa.

Consider a task in your project that is running behind schedule. You could bring in additional workers to speed up progress, but this would increase labor costs. On the other hand, you could extend the timeline to complete the task with the existing team, but this would delay the overall project completion.

Analyzing these tradeoff scenarios helps you understand the implications of adjusting time or cost, allowing you to make strategic decisions that best align with your project goals.

Making Informed Decisions

Once you've analyzed the tradeoff scenarios, the next step is to make informed decisions. This involves choosing the best course of action based on your project objectives, constraints, and stakeholder expectations.

If completing the project on time is the top priority, you might invest additional resources to speed up progress, even if it incurs a higher cost. However, if keeping the project within budget is more important, you might extend the timeline instead.

Making these decisions requires careful consideration, clear communication with stakeholders, and a keen understanding of your project's priorities.

Monitoring and Adjusting Tradeoffs

The consideration between time and cost doesn't end with deciding—it continues throughout the project. As the project progresses, you need to monitor the impact of your decisions and adjust the tradeoffs as required.

Monitoring involves paying close attention to the project's timeline and budget and checking if the progress matches your plans. You must identify the cause and take corrective action if you notice any discrepancies.

For example, suppose a task takes longer than planned despite the extra resources. In that case, you might need to reevaluate your plan, provide additional training to workers, or revise your timeline or budget.

On the other hand, adjusting tradeoffs involves revisiting your decisions in light of new information or changes in the project. If new challenges arise or project priorities change, you might need to reassess the time-cost tradeoffs and make new decisions.

In construction management, mastering time-cost tradeoff analysis is essential. It's comparable to finely adjusting the components of your construction project to strike the right balance between time and cost. By honing this skill, you ensure your project aligns with objectives and meets stakeholder expectations.

Use these insights from this chapter as a guide to navigate project complexities, make informed decisions, and achieve successful outcomes.

In construction management, every decision matters, every action counts, and every project can be a success. So, let's continue learning, growing, and building a successful path forward.

5

FINANCIAL MANAGEMENT IN CONSTRUCTION

IMAGINE BALANCING ON A TIGHTROPE, high above a bustling cityscape. With each step, you must maintain perfect equilibrium, shifting your weight subtly to counteract the changing winds. In construction management, financial management is similar to this thrilling tightrope walk. It's about maintaining a delicate balance between various costs, ensuring the project stays within budget while delivering the desired results.

As we step onto this financial tightrope, let's arm ourselves with the right techniques to maintain our balance. Let's start with cost estimation, a critical first step in financial management that lays the foundation for all subsequent decisions.

COST ESTIMATION TECHNIQUES

Cost estimation is like plotting your course before going on a road trip. It involves predicting the costs of a construction project and providing a roadmap for budgeting, bidding, and financial planning. Several techniques are used in cost estimation, each with its unique approach and application.

Unit Cost Estimating

Unit cost estimating is similar to shopping for groceries with a per-item budget. It involves determining the cost of a single unit of work and then multiplying it by the quantity required.

For example, if you're building a brick wall, you'd calculate the cost of laying one brick, including the costs of the brick, mortar, and labor. Then, multiply this unit cost by the bricks required to get the total cost. This straightforward technique makes it a popular choice for simple projects or initial estimates.

Parametric Estimating

Parametric estimating is like predicting a car's fuel consumption based on its mileage rate and the distance of the journey. It involves using statistical modeling and historical data to predict the cost of a project.

Let's say you're building a series of similar houses. From previous projects, you know the average cost per square foot. You can then multiply this rate by the size of each house to get a rough estimate of the cost. This technique is useful when you have reliable historical data, and the current project is similar in nature.

Bottom-Up Estimating

Bottom-up estimating is like connecting the dots, where each dot represents a task in the project. It involves estimating the cost of each individual task and then adding them up to get the total cost.

If you're constructing a commercial building, you will break down the project into tasks like site preparation, foundation work, framing, roofing, etc. Then, you'd estimate the cost of each task, considering the labor, materials, and equipment required. Finally, you'd add up these costs to get the total project cost. This technique is time-consuming but provides a detailed and accurate estimate, making it ideal for complex projects.

Analogous Estimating

Analogous estimating is like predicting the duration of a movie based on the length of similar movies you've watched before. It involves using the cost of similar past projects to estimate the cost of the current project.

For instance, if you've previously built a residential complex with similar specifications to a new project, you could use the cost of the past project as a baseline for the new one, adjusting for any differences in scale or complexity. This technique is quick and easy, but its accuracy depends on the similarity between the projects and the reliability of past data.

Each cost estimation technique offers a unique perspective, like different lenses through which we can view our project's financial landscape. They give us the tools to plot our course on the financial tightrope, helping us maintain our balance and navigate toward successful project completion. As we continue, remember that cost estimation is not a one-size-fits-all process. It's a toolkit from which we choose the right tool for the job, tailored to the project's needs, complexity, and stage of development.

So, whether you're laying bricks for a wall or planning a high-rise, remember to choose wisely, estimate carefully, and always keep your eyes on the financial horizon. After all, balancing the books is not just about numbers; it's about strategy, foresight, and the careful management of resources. It's about walking the financial tightrope confidently, ensuring every step, shift, and move brings you closer to your project goals.

BUDGETING AND COST CONTROL STRATEGIES

Developing a Budget

Examining the financial aspects of a construction project, the initial focus is on the budget—a comprehensive outline detailing the expected costs of various project components. This financial framework outlines the economic structure of your construction undertaking.

Developing this framework requires a detailed breakdown of your project into individual tasks; each assigned its corresponding cost. These tasks encompass everything from site preparation and material acquisition to labor and equipment expenses. Each cost factor is meticulously estimated and aggregated to determine the overall project budget.

The budget is a benchmark against which the actual project expenses are compared. It is a tool for guiding financial decisions, managing expenditures, and maintaining the project's economic viability.

Implementing Cost Control Measures

With the budget in place, our financial roadmap's next step is establishing cost control measures. These measures are the brakes on our financial vehicle, ensuring we maintain a safe speed and don't overshoot our budget.

Cost control measures are procedures and guidelines designed to monitor expenses and prevent cost overruns. They involve setting cost targets for various project stages, establishing approval processes for expenditures, and defining procedures for handling changes that impact cost.

For instance, a cost control measure could be a rule that the project manager must approve any expenditure exceeding a certain threshold. Another measure could be a process for reviewing and approving change orders to ensure they don't inflate the project cost without justification.

Tracking and Reviewing Costs

Cost control measures are useless if they aren't paired with diligent cost tracking and review. This is the financial radar of our project, constantly scanning the horizon for any deviations from the budget.

Cost tracking involves recording all project expenditures as they occur and comparing them against the budgeted costs. This could be done using accounting software, spreadsheets, or specialized project management tools.

On the other hand, the review process involves analyzing these costs to identify trends, isolate problem areas, and assess the project's financial health. Regular cost reviews provide valuable insights into how effectively the budget is managed and where adjustments may be needed.

Adjusting Budgets as Needed

Our financial examination doesn't end with tracking and review. As the project evolves, so does our budget. Adjusting the budget is like recalibrating our financial compass, ensuring it stays aligned with the project's changing landscape.

Budget adjustments may be needed due to unforeseen circumstances, changes in project scope, or variations in material or labor costs. These adjustments are not signs of poor planning; they are indicative of a proactive approach to financial management.

When adjusting the budget, it's essential to maintain transparent communication with stakeholders, explaining the reasons for the adjustments and their impact on the project. This openness helps build trust, fosters understanding, and ensures everyone stays on the same financial page.

In the expansive realm of construction management, financial management takes center stage. It requires precision, vigilance, and adaptability—an aspect that demands careful consideration of costs aligning with the budget and constructing a financial perspective that ensures success. As we navigate this intricate process, we understand that financial management extends beyond mere numbers; it encompasses strategy, foresight, and balance. This equilibrium converts our journey through the economic blueprint into a well-coordinated construction project, guiding us toward the successful completion of our project.

CASH FLOW MANAGEMENT IN CONSTRUCTION

Projecting Cash Flow

In the operational structure of construction, projecting cash flow is similar to planning the financial aspects of our project. It offers a preview into the future, outlining the expected inflows and outflows of cash throughout the project's timeline.

This anticipation begins with thoroughly examining the project plan and evaluating each task for its anticipated costs and revenues. It involves predicting when payments for labor, materials, and equipment will be required and when client payments will be received. This projection serves as a financial plan, guiding the timing and magnitude of our cash transactions.

Consider the scenario of a commercial building project. During the excavation and foundation phase, substantial expenditures may be incurred for site preparation and concrete work. Recognizing this in your cash flow projection enables you to ensure adequate funds are available during this crucial early stage.

Tracking Cash Inflows and Outflows

Armed with our cash flow projection, we assume the role of a vigilant financial overseer, closely monitoring the actual cash inflows and outflows. This continuous oversight ensures that our financial performance aligns with the plan and that any deviations are promptly identified and addressed.

The monitoring process involves meticulous record-keeping of each financial transaction, comparing the actual cash flows with the projected amounts. It entails regularly updating our cash flow projection with real data, transforming it from a static document into a dynamic financial tool.

For example, if a supplier provides an unexpected discount on materials, resulting in a lower-than-projected cash outflow, acknowledging and incorporating this into the cash flow projection will uphold its accuracy and utility.

Overseeing Payment Schedules

In the financial dynamics of our project, payment schedules establish the tempo. They govern the timing of cash inflows and outflows, influencing the ebb and flow of cash flow. Managing these schedules is pivotal for sustaining a positive cash flow and preventing financial constraints.

Effective payment schedule management entails collaborating with clients, contractors, suppliers, and other stakeholders to align payment terms with the project's cash flow requirements. It involves negotiating favorable terms, such as early payment discounts or extended credit periods, and ensuring timely payments.

Consider a scenario where a substantial equipment rental payment is due just before a significant client payment is anticipated. Negotiating an extension with the rental company can circumvent a temporary cash shortage and maintain a positive cash flow.

Securing Liquidity

The concluding phase in our cash flow management endeavors is securing liquidity. Liquidity serves as the life force of a construction project, ensuring that ample cash is accessible to meet financial commitments as they arise.

Securing liquidity involves maintaining a reserve of readily available funds, often in a cash reserve or an accessible line of credit. This financial safety net is crucial for addressing unforeseen expenses, compensating for delays in payment reception, or seizing sudden opportunities.

For instance, if a rare chance arises to procure bulk materials at a considerable discount, having liquidity enables you to capitalize on this opportunity, potentially yielding long-term cost savings.

In the comprehensive performance of construction management, cash flow management assumes a leading role. It shapes the financial storyline of our project, guiding decisions, influencing actions, and ultimately determining the project's economic success. As we navigate the dynamic field of construction management, let's bear in mind that maintaining a positive cash flow entails more than just numerical considerations—it involves planning, monitoring, effective management, and assurance. It's about finding the right equilibrium between inflows and outflows, judiciously timing payments, and consistently focusing on liquidity. Armed with these capabilities, we can ensure that our construction projects stand resilient in concrete and steel and their financial foundations.

UNDERSTANDING AND MANAGING CONSTRUCTION CONTRACTS

Contracts are the backbone of the construction industry, serving as binding agreements that outline the rights and responsibilities of all involved parties. They function as rulebooks, ensuring everyone adheres to agreed-upon terms and fulfills their designated roles.

Various types of construction contracts cater to diverse projects and circumstances:

- **Fixed Price Contracts**: Also known as lump-sum contracts, these agreements establish a fixed total price for all construction activities. The contractor bears the risk, committing to completing the work within the agreed-upon price, irrespective of actual costs.
- **Cost Plus Contracts**: In these agreements, the owner covers actual construction costs plus an additional fee for the

contractor. This fee may be a fixed amount or a percentage of costs, incentivizing the contractor to control expenses.

- **Time and Material Contracts**: These flexible agreements involve the owner paying the contractor based on time and materials used. They're suitable for projects with uncertain or likely changing scopes.
- **Unit Pricing Contracts**: The contractor receives a specific amount for each completed work unit, such as per square foot or cubic yard. They're employed in projects with large scopes or repetitive tasks.

Key elements in every contract include:

- **Scope of Work**: Describing tasks, materials, and standards, this section defines the contractor's obligations and owner's expectations.
- **Payment Terms**: Outline how and when the contractor receives payment, including details about progress payments, retainage, and conditions for final payment.
- **Change Order Clause**: Specifying how changes to the scope of work will be handled, including the process for approving changes and adjusting the contract price.
- **Dispute Resolution**: Establishing procedures for resolving disagreements, such as mediation, arbitration, or litigation.

Effective contract management involves monitoring performance, documenting progress, and addressing issues promptly. Proactive communication through regular meetings and progress reports fosters understanding and builds trust among parties.

When disputes arise, reviewing the contract, understanding each party's rights and obligations, and open communication can often resolve issues amicably. The dispute resolution clause guides the next steps involving mediation, arbitration, or litigation if needed.

Contracts play a pivotal role in construction management, dictating roles and guiding projects from start to finish. Successful navigation of construction contracts requires a clear understanding, careful management, and a commitment to fairness and integrity. It's a dance of responsibility and cooperation, shaping the success of every construction project.

In the upcoming chapter, we will explore the intricacies of risk management, analyzing potential challenges and pitfalls inherent in construction projects. We will focus on proactive strategies to anticipate and effectively mitigate these risks.

6

RISK MANAGEMENT IN CONSTRUCTION

IN CONSTRUCTION MANAGEMENT, a project leader must navigate the challenging terrain of risks and uncertainties. Risk management is not an option; it's a necessity. It acts as our guiding compass through unexpected challenges and an anchor amidst unforeseen events, distinguishing between a smoothly sailing project and one that encounters complications.

In this chapter, we'll explore the extensive realm of risk management, charting our course through identifying and assessing risks. We'll take command of the situation with mitigation and contingency plans, fortify our project with the right insurance, and master the art of change management. So, let's educate ourselves and forge ahead into Risk Management.

IDENTIFYING AND ASSESSING RISKS

Risk Identification Techniques

Risk identification is very important no matter what size of construction project you are managing. It involves spotting risks that could impact our project, ranging from unexpected cost increases and delays to safety issues and quality problems. Various techniques aid in risk identification, such as brainstorming and the SWOT analysis, which provides a comprehensive view of internal and external risks.

The SWOT analysis is a strategic planning tool used by construction companies to identify and assess the strengths and weaknesses of a team or a project, in addition to potential opportunities or threats.

The acronym SWOT stands for:

- **Strengths:** Internal factors that give an organization an advantage over others. These could include a strong brand, skilled workforce, or advanced technology.
- **Weaknesses:** Internal factors that may place an organization at a disadvantage. Examples include outdated technology, lack of skilled personnel, or poor management.
- **Opportunities:** External factors that the organization could exploit to its advantage. Opportunities might include emerging markets, technological advancements, or changes in consumer behavior.
- **Threats:** External factors that could pose challenges or risks to the organization. Threats might include economic downturns, increased competition, or regulatory changes.

By analyzing these four elements, companies providing critical path construction work can develop strategies to capitalize on their strengths, address their weaknesses, take advantage of opportunities, and mitigate potential threats. SWOT analysis is a valuable tool for strategic planning, decision-making, and understanding the overall position of an organization in its competitive environment.

Risk Assessment Methods

Once potential risks are spotted, our next step is to assess their potential impact, like estimating the size of a challenge on the horizon and determining how much it could affect our project. Standard methods for risk assessment include the risk matrix, evaluating risks based on potential impact and likelihood, and the risk register, which serves as a central repository of risk information.

Prioritizing Risks

After assessing risks, we prioritize them, much like deciding which challenges to address first, based on their significance and proximity. Risks with a high potential impact and likelihood of occurrence are addressed first, as they pose significant threats that could significantly disrupt our project. On the other hand, risks with low impact and low probability can be handled later.

Documenting Risks

As we identify, assess, and prioritize risks, it's crucial to document our findings, much like charting our course on a map, leaving a trail for others to follow. Clear, comprehensive, and accessible risk documentation includes details about each risk, its potential impact and likelihood, and mitigation strategies. This documentation serves as a valuable reference for the team.

For instance, in commercial building construction, identifying the risk of material price fluctuations would involve documenting its potential impact on the project budget, the probability of occurrence based on market trends, and mitigation strategies like locking prices with suppliers or allocating a contingency in the budget. This documentation keeps the team informed and prepared.

In the vast construction management arena, risks are the challenges that test our journey. We confidently navigate by identifying, assessing, prioritizing, and documenting these risks. We steer our project through uncertainty, ensuring it stays on course and moves towards success. As you guide your project through the challenges of risks and uncertainties, remain vigilant, prepared, and confident. With the right tools and techniques, you can navigate any challenge and guide your project safely to its destination.

The following section will explore risk management further, providing strategies and techniques for mitigating risks, planning contingencies, and ensuring our project is well-equipped to handle any challenges.

MITIGATION AND CONTINGENCY PLANNING

In the complex landscape of construction management, risk mitigation, and contingency planning are the strategically coordinated actions that maintain the operational flow. They constitute the tactical sequence, enabling us to foresee possible challenges, strategize our responses, and stay adaptable in unforeseen circumstances. Let's delve into these essential steps in managing risk.

Crafting Risk Mitigation Strategies

Risk mitigation is the carefully constructed framework that directs our efforts to diminish risks' impact or likelihood. It involves strategically planning actions to either sidestep the risk entirely or reduce its potential harm.

Imagine a situation where the project risks delays due to adverse weather conditions. A risk mitigation strategy might include scheduling weather-sensitive tasks during a season with typically favorable weather or investing in weather-protective equipment or materials to reduce the potential for weather-related delays.

The crux of effective risk mitigation lies in customizing strategies to the specific nature and context of each risk. It entails grasping the intricacies of the risk, exploring potential interventions, and selecting the most efficient and feasible strategies.

Crafting Contingency Plans

Despite our best efforts at risk mitigation, certain risks may still materialize. This is where contingency plans come into play. They serve as our backup plans, the alternative steps we've devised in case our original maneuvers face disruptions.

A contingency plan delineates the actions to be taken if a specific risk event occurs. For example, suppose there's a risk of a critical supplier failing to deliver materials on time. In that case, the contingency plan might involve sourcing the materials from an alternative supplier, adjusting the construction schedule, or modifying the design to use different materials.

Developing effective contingency plans requires a thorough understanding of the risk, a clear definition of the trigger conditions that will activate the plan, and a detailed outline of the response actions.

Executing Mitigation Measures

With our risk mitigation strategies and contingency plans in place, the next step is to implement these plans. This is the performance phase, where our carefully orchestrated moves are brought to life on the stage of our construction project.

Executing mitigation measures involves integrating these actions into the project plan, allocating resources, and assigning responsibilities. It's about ensuring that the planned measures are executed effectively, monitored continuously, and adjusted as needed for maximum effectiveness.

For example, if a mitigation strategy involves training the team in a new construction technique to reduce the risk of errors, the implementation would include scheduling the training, providing the necessary resources, and assigning a team member to oversee the process.

Reviewing and Updating Plans

In the ever-evolving construction process, our moves must adapt to the changing rhythm of risks. As the project progresses, new risks may emerge, existing risks may change, and our mitigation and contingency plans may need to be updated.

Reviewing and updating plans involves regular risk reassessments, monitoring the effectiveness of mitigation measures, and refining the plans based on these insights. It's about maintaining the relevance and effectiveness of our risk management efforts in the dynamic construction environment.

For instance, if a new risk emerges during the project, such as a change in regulatory requirements, the risk management plan would need to be updated with this risk, along with appropriate mitigation strategies and contingency plans.

In the intricate landscape of construction management, risk mitigation, and contingency planning are the strategic maneuvers that keep the project moving smoothly. These steps form a sequence that allows us to anticipate potential challenges, plan our responses, and remain adaptable to unexpected events. With these strategies in place, we can confidently navigate the complexities of risk, ensuring our construction projects progress toward success.

THE ROLE OF INSURANCE IN RISK MANAGEMENT

In the dynamic field of construction management, insurance acts as a safety net, ready to catch us if uncertainties lead to stumbles. It provides reassurance that, even when risks materialize, we are shielded from catastrophic losses.

Types of Construction Insurance

On the expansive stage of construction, diverse types of insurance play specific roles, each addressing different risks associated with the project.

- **Builder's Risk Insurance**: Also known as course of construction insurance, it safeguards the construction project. This coverage extends to damage or loss of building materials, equipment, and structure during construction caused by events such as fire, theft, or natural disasters.

- **General Liability Insurance**: This comprehensive coverage protects against legal actions from property damage, injury, or accidents on the construction site. It is the leading insurance policy, offering extensive coverage for common liabilities.
- **Professional Liability Insurance**: Often referred to as Errors and Omissions (E&O) Insurance, it covers claims related to negligent acts, errors, or omissions occurring while providing professional services. Design-build firms offering both construction and professional services find this insurance particularly relevant.
- **Workers' Compensation Insurance**: Mandatory in most jurisdictions, this coverage protects employees injured on the job. It covers medical expenses and lost wages, ensuring the well-being of the construction crew and any project's lifeblood.

Assessing Insurance Needs

Similar to how a director selects the right tools for a construction project, a construction manager must choose the appropriate insurance coverage. This selection process, known as risk assessment, involves identifying potential risks, evaluating their potential impact, and determining the types of insurance that can mitigate them.

For instance, if a project involves a high degree of technical design work, Professional Liability Insurance would be crucial to cover potential design errors or omissions. On the other hand, a project with a large construction crew would require a robust Workers' Compensation policy.

Understanding Policy Terms

An insurance policy is a complex document with terms and conditions dictating coverage. It's crucial to understand these terms, much like a professional needs to comprehend the details of a technical paper.

Key terms include the policy limit, the maximum amount the insurer will pay for a covered loss, and the deductible, which is the amount the policyholder must pay out-of-pocket before the insurance kicks in. Exclusions, specific situations, or damages not covered by the policy are also critical to understand.

Claim Management

In the event of a loss or damage, the claim management process is the final stage in the insurance performance. It's reporting the loss to the insurance company, providing necessary documentation, and collaborating with the insurer to settle the claim.

Effective claim management involves prompt reporting of incidents, thorough documentation of damages, and clear communication with the insurance company. It's about ensuring that legitimate claims are settled quickly and fairly, enabling the project to get back on track with minimal disruption.

In construction management, insurance plays a crucial role in risk management. It provides a safety net, protecting projects from the financial impact of unexpected events. As we navigate the uncertainties of construction, understanding the types of insurance, assessing our insurance needs, understanding policy terms, and managing claims effectively can provide the reassurance we need to keep our projects on course toward success.

DEALING WITH UNFORESEEN EVENTS AND CHANGES

Change Management Process

In the dynamic construction arena, change is a constant companion. Changes are bound to occur, whether it's a design alteration, a budget adjustment, or a schedule modification. Managing these changes effectively is critical to maintaining the project's trajectory and avoiding unnecessary disruptions.

The change management process is a systematic approach to handling changes in a project. It begins with recognizing the need for a change. This could be triggered by a client's request, a regulatory requirement, an unforeseen issue, or a strategic decision.

Next is the evaluation stage, where the impact of the proposed change is analyzed. This involves understanding how the change would impact the project's cost, schedule, quality, and other vital aspects. It's about determining whether the change is beneficial and feasible.

Once the change is approved, it's time for implementation. This involves making the necessary adjustments in the project plan, informing all stakeholders, and executing the change. It's about turning the plan into action and ensuring the change is smoothly integrated into the project.

Handling Unexpected Events

In the course of a construction project, various unexpected events can occur. These could range from adverse weather conditions and equipment breakdowns to labor shortages and unforeseen site conditions.

Handling these unexpected events involves swift decision-making, effective communication, and flexible planning. It's about assessing the situation, exploring possible solutions, and deciding on the best course of action.

For instance, if an unexpected storm hits the construction site, you may need to halt work to ensure the safety of your crew. You would then need to communicate the situation to all stakeholders, adjust the project schedule, and plan for resuming work once conditions improve.

Managing Change Orders

Change orders are formal documents that outline changes to the original contract. They are common in construction projects, providing a mechanism to accommodate scope, schedule, or cost changes.

Managing change orders involves carefully reviewing the proposed changes, thoroughly analyzing their impact, and communicating clearly with all parties involved. It's about ensuring the change is justified, its effects are understood, and all agree upon its implementation.

For example, if a change order is issued to add a new feature to the building, you must evaluate how this change would affect the project's cost, schedule, and other aspects. You would then discuss these impacts with the client and revise the project plan to incorporate the change once an agreement is reached.

Lessons Learned Analysis

Every construction project's unique challenges and experiences provide valuable lessons. Conducting a lessons-learned analysis at the end of a project or after significant events is a way to capture and use these insights for future projects.

This analysis involves reflecting on what went well, what could have been done differently, and what lessons can be drawn from the experience. It's about turning hindsight into foresight, transforming past experiences into future improvements.

For instance, if a project experienced delays due to frequent equipment breakdowns, one lesson learned might be to invest in better maintenance practices or to keep backup equipment on hand. By documenting and applying these lessons, you can continually improve your management practices and enhance the success of future projects.

In the exciting world of construction management, dealing with changes and unexpected events is part of the game. It's about staying agile amidst uncertainties, managing changes effectively, and learning from each experience. This adaptability helps us steer our projects through the dynamic seas of construction, ensuring that we stay on course, weather any storm, and reach our destination successfully. As we continue to explore the world of construction management, let's carry these lessons forward, helping us navigate the challenges and seize the opportunities that lie ahead.

In the next chapter, we will focus on the practical application of our learnings, exploring real-life examples of successful construction management. We'll look closer at the strategies, techniques, and insights that have shaped these successes, providing a practical perspective to complement our theoretical understanding. So, prepare for a look into the real construction management world.

7

STORIES FROM THE JOBSITE: RESIDENTIAL CONSTRUCTION MANAGEMENT

IMAGINE A TEAM PREPARING TOOLS, testing processes, adjusting parameters, and refining coordination. That's what planning a construction project feels like. A meticulous alignment of elements - time, cost, quality, and scope - converging to ensure a successful outcome. This systematic cooperation begins with the project's planning phase.

PROJECT OVERVIEW AND PLANNING PHASE

Defining Project Objectives

Similar to a wedding planner outlining the tone and theme of a wedding, setting accurate, hands-on project objectives provides clarity and purpose to your construction endeavor. It involves precisely detailing what you intend to accomplish—constructing a two-story residential house, renovating a kitchen, or adding a new extension to an existing structure.

The objectives should adhere to the SMART criteria: specific, measurable, achievable, relevant, and time-bound. For example, a SMART objective for residential house construction could be:

"Construct a 2000 square feet, three-bedroom house in Springfield within a budget of $300,000, aiming for completion in 12 months."

Developing the Project Scope

Once the objectives are established, the subsequent phase is to craft the project scope. Consider this as the blueprint for your project. The project scope comprehensively depicts the activities essential to achieve the project objectives. It delineates the tasks, resources needed, and the anticipated outcomes at the project's conclusion.

For a residential house project, the scope may encompass site preparation, foundation work, framing, roofing, interior finishing, and landscaping. It might also stipulate the quality standards, materials, and the timeline associated with each task.

Creating the Work Breakdown Structure

The work breakdown structure (WBS) functions as the foundational structure of your project, breaking down the intricate composition into manageable components.

In a residential construction project, the WBS might start at the highest level with the project title (e.g., "Springfield House Construction"), then break down into phases (e.g., "Foundation," "Superstructure," "Finishes"), and further break down into individual tasks (e.g., "Excavation," "Concrete Pouring," "Bricklaying").

Establishing the Project Schedule

With the WBS in place, the next step is establishing the project schedule - which ultimately is the entire flow of your construction project. This involves assigning start and end dates to each task, considering their sequence and dependencies.

For instance, in a residential construction project, you can't start the roofing until the framing is complete. So, "Framing" should be scheduled before "Roofing." And if "Framing" is expected to end on June 30th, "Roofing" would start on July 1st.

Creating a Gantt chart can be especially useful here. It provides a visual representation of the project schedule, allowing everyone to see the timing of different tasks at a glance.

Preparing the Budget

Finally, like the construction manager ensuring that no cost element overshadows another, preparing the budget ensures that no actual construction costs outweigh the others. It involves estimating the cost of each task and adding them up to form the total project cost.

In a residential construction project, the budget might include costs for land acquisition, permits and fees, labor, materials, equipment, and an allowance for contingencies. Each of these costs must be carefully estimated and tracked to ensure the project stays within budget.

The planning phase is the fine-tuning process of our construction project, a critical period of aligning elements, setting the pace, and finalizing the essential details that might adversely affect the project. It's about laying the groundwork for a successful project and setting up the job site for the maze of construction elements to fall into place. So, as we start on our construction project, let's ensure we invest ample time and effort in planning, for the planning and coordination make the project come together piece by piece with the anticipation of assured construction success.

EXECUTION AND CONTROL PHASE

Managing Project Resources

The person in charge of the construction project is the project manager, who directs the allocation of subcontractors, labor, and resources, ensuring each one is on-site as needed to fulfill its role. These resources include the workforce, construction materials, and essential equipment.

Aside from overseeing the construction manager and a well-coordinated project, the project manager must synchronize these components, guaranteeing the timely presence of the appropriate workforce, the punctual delivery of materials, and the readiness of equipment for deployment. This synchronization minimizes downtime, prevents delays, and encourages the efficient utilization of resources.

Imagine the process of assembling the walls of a residential building. The project manager ensures that the masons are scheduled to work precisely when bricks and mortar arrive, and the mortar mixer is prepared for action. This careful coordination provides a seamless workflow without interruptions, sustaining the project's momentum.

Quality Control Measures

In the construction world, quality isn't overlooked; it's a habit woven into every task and every action. It's the standard to ensure a construction project hits all the right milestones and specifications, creating a building that may be standing for centuries.

Quality control in construction involves setting standards for each task, monitoring work to ensure these standards are met, and taking corrective action when deviations occur. It's about maintaining a keen eye for detail, ensuring the construction work aligns with the design specifications and meets the required quality standards.

Take, for instance, the task of installing electrical wiring. The project manager ensures the electricians follow the correct procedures, use the appropriate materials, and adhere to safety standards. Regular inspections and testing confirm the quality of work, and any issues found are promptly corrected.

Monitoring Project Progress

To keep the construction project progressing in a timely manner, the project manager must keep a steady pace of installation, tracking the project's progress and adjusting the speed as needed. This process involves comparing actual progress against the planned schedule, identifying any delays or issues, and taking corrective action.

For example, if the house's framing is falling behind schedule, the project manager identifies the cause of the delay, such as a shortage of labor or materials. The project manager then takes corrective action, like bringing in additional workers or expediting material delivery, to get the project back on track.

Implementing Change Orders

As is pretty typical in construction, change is as inevitable as the setting sun at the end of a day. Change orders are formal requests for alterations to the project, whether it's an addition, deletion, or modification in the scope of work.

When a change order arises, the project manager carefully reviews the request, assesses its impact on the project's cost, schedule, and quality, and decides whether to approve it. If approved, the change is seamlessly woven into the project plan, with adjustments to the schedule, budget, and resource allocation as needed.

For instance, if a client requests an upgrade in flooring materials, the project manager calculates the additional cost and time required, communicates this to the client, and coordinates the procurement of the new materials and the rescheduling of the flooring work upon approval.

Risk Management Strategies

Leading a construction project through uncertain situations requires a solid plan to handle potential problems. It's like using a compass to navigate the project through challenges. This means spotting possible construction-related issues, figuring out how much they might affect the project and how likely they will happen, and developing practical solutions.

These responses could be risk avoidance, where the project plan is adjusted to evade the risk entirely, or risk mitigation, where actions are taken to reduce the risk's impact or likelihood. In some cases, where the risk's impact is minor, the strategy might be risk acceptance, where the risk is acknowledged, but no proactive action is taken unless it occurs.

For example, if there's a risk of material price fluctuations, the project manager might lock in prices with suppliers or allocate a contingency in the budget to cover potential increases. This proactive approach ensures the project remains prepared for uncertainties, ready to weather any storm.

OVERCOMING CHALLENGES

Dealing with Unforeseen Site Conditions

In the big picture of construction, a construction site is the groundwork where we build our project, but this groundwork often hides unexpected challenges. Unforeseen construction site issues, like unusable soils, unnoticed water issues, or buried hazardous materials, can mess up even the most carefully laid out plans.

We encountered a hidden rock formation during excavation in our residential construction project. This unexpected obstacle could have delayed our project and inflated costs. But instead of letting it derail us, we saw it as an opportunity to showcase some problem-solving skills.

Our first step was to call in a geotechnical engineer to assess the situation. Based on their findings, we adjusted our excavation strategy to safely remove the rock without compromising the site's stability. This proactive approach allowed us to overcome the challenge without significant delays or cost overruns.

Managing Changes in Project Scope

The fluid nature of construction projects means that changes are inevitable. A client may request additional features or an inspector may require modifications for code compliance. Managing these changes in the project scope is critical to maintaining control over the timeline and budget.

In our project, mid-way through construction, the client decided to add a basement. This significant change required a reassessment of our project plan and budget. We carefully evaluated the impact of this addition, considering factors like additional excavation, reinforcement, and waterproofing needs.

We then communicated these changes to the client, discussing additional costs and time requirements. Once they agreed, we revised our project plan and schedule to accommodate the new basement. This transparency and flexibility allowed us to manage the change effectively, keeping our project on track despite the added complexity.

Resolving Conflicts Among Team Members

A construction project is a collaborative effort, bringing together a diverse team of professionals. However, diversity can conflict. Resolving conflicts among team members is crucial to maintaining a positive work environment and ensuring project success.

On our project, a conflict arose between the plumbing and electrical teams over scheduling. Both teams needed to work in the same space, leading to disagreements over who should go first. Left unresolved, this conflict could have caused delays and affected work quality.

To address the issue, we facilitated a team meeting to discuss their concerns and find a solution. We developed a shared schedule that satisfied both teams by promoting open communication and encouraging collaboration. This swift conflict resolution ensured our project continued smoothly, with team morale intact.

Overcoming Delays in Material Supply

Timely delivery of construction materials is a critical aspect of project management. Delays in material supply can stall progress, leading to cost overruns and schedule extensions.

Our project faced a significant challenge when a major supplier failed to deliver bricks on time. Rather than letting this delay halt our progress, we sprang into action. We contacted alternative suppliers and secured the necessary bricks without a significant delay.

This experience underscored the importance of having backup plans and maintaining solid relationships with multiple suppliers. By remaining flexible and responsive, we overcame this challenge and kept our project moving forward.

Navigating Regulatory Compliance Issues

Every construction project operates within a framework of building codes, zoning laws, and environmental regulations. Navigating these regulatory compliance issues can be complex, but ensuring the project's legality and safety is crucial.

Midway through our project, a new building regulation came into effect, requiring additional insulation for energy efficiency. Initially, this seemed like a setback. However, we saw it as an opportunity to improve our project's sustainability.

We quickly revised our plans to incorporate the additional insulation and worked with the building inspector to ensure compliance. While this change did result in a minor cost increase, it also improved the energy efficiency of the home – a valuable selling point for the client.

Challenges are par for the course in the often fast-paced world of construction management. They test our resilience, stretch our problem-solving skills, and ultimately, shape us into better project managers. By facing these challenges head-on and overcoming them, we ensure our projects reach successful completion and embody the values of resilience, adaptation, and excellence.

KEY TAKEAWAYS AND LESSONS LEARNED

Importance of Detailed Planning

A key lesson learned from our residential construction project is the critical role that detailed planning plays in the project's success. Think of it as the blueprint guiding all project activities' raceway. Careful planning is like a roadmap that outlines the path to be taken, the milestones to be achieved, and the resources to be utilized.

Detailed planning additionally involves breaking down the project into distinct, manageable tasks, each with a clear goal, timeline, and assignee for each task. It's about foreseeing potential challenges, planning for contingencies, and setting up mechanisms for monitoring and controlling the project's progress.

In the residential construction project, detailed planning helped us coordinate activities efficiently, manage resources effectively, and stay on top of project progress. It provided a clear vision of the project objectives and the steps needed to achieve them, paving the way for a smooth and successful project execution.

Value of Effective Communication

Another crucial takeaway from our project is the immense value of effective communication in managing construction projects. Communication is the thread that weaves together the various elements of a project, ensuring they work in harmony towards the collective goal.

Effective communication involves sharing relevant information promptly and clearly with all project stakeholders. It's about fostering an environment of transparency, where everyone understands their roles, responsibilities, and the expectations placed on them.

Our project's regular meetings, progress reports, and open communication channels enabled us to maintain clear and consistent communication. This helped to avoid misunderstandings, quickly resolve issues, and keep everyone aligned with the project objectives.

Proactive Risk Management

The residential construction project also underscored proactive risk management's necessity to ensure project success. Risk management is the shield that guards a project against potential threats and uncertainties.

Proactive risk management involves identifying potential risks, assessing their impact and likelihood, and planning appropriate responses. It's about anticipating challenges before they arise and implementing strategies to mitigate their effects.

In the project, proactive risk management allowed us to anticipate potential issues, from unexpected site conditions to changes in project scope, and devise effective strategies to manage them. This helped us to keep the project on track despite the uncertainties, underscoring the crucial role of risk management in construction projects.

Quality Control and Project Success

Finally, the project highlighted the pivotal role of quality control in ensuring project success. Quality control is the yardstick that measures the project's output against the set standards, ensuring that the final product meets the expectations of quality and performance.

Quality control in a construction project involves setting standards for each task, closely monitoring the work to ensure these standards are met, and taking corrective action when deviations occur. It's about maintaining a keen eye for detail and refusing to compromise on the quality of work.

In our residential construction project, stringent quality control measures ensured that every task, from excavation to finishing, was executed to the highest standards. This resulted in a high-quality end product and enhanced stakeholder satisfaction, reinforcing the importance of quality control in construction projects.

As we move forward in our introduction to construction management, let's not forget these valuable lessons. They remind us that detailed planning, effective communication, proactive risk management, and stringent quality control are the foundation of every successful construction project. As we prepare to delve deeper into construction management, let's take these lessons with us, using them as guiding principles in our pursuit of excellence in construction management.

Next, let's take our learning further as we read about real-life commercial and industrial construction management examples in the coming chapters. The lessons we've learned from our residential construction project will be our benchmark as we explore these new terrains. So, let's keep building on our knowledge, expanding our perspectives, and fine-tuning our path toward success in construction management.

8

STORIES FROM THE JOBSITE: COMMERCIAL CONTSTRUCTION MANAGEMENT

IMAGINE THIS: The morning sun is just starting to illuminate the horizon as a team of construction workers embarks on their day. A building begins to take shape amid the buzzing machinery and clattering tools. As a skilled coordinator, the project manager directs this intricate dance, juggling various components. Welcome to commercial construction management—a domain where precision and teamwork converge to craft something exceptional.

In this chapter, we'll dive into managing commercial construction. We'll give you a peek behind the scenes of an actual commercial construction project, sharing details about how it's planned and carried out, the obstacles faced and conquered, and the essential things to remember and learn. So, let's not waste any time—gear up with our work boots and hard hats and head to the busy construction site of a commercial building.

PROJECT OVERVIEW AND PLANNING PHASE

Defining Project Goals

At the beginning of a project, defining clear and specific goals is like setting the wheels in motion to gain momentum for the project. Our commercial project aimed to construct a modern, energy-efficient office building within a set budget and timeline. This goal was our collaborative effort, helping us concentrate on planning and decision-making and ensuring everyone involved was working towards the same objective.

Identifying Stakeholders

Like every pro baseball player has a crucial role on a baseball team, every stakeholder contributes significantly to a construction project. For our office building project, the stakeholders included the client who commissioned the project, the architects who designed the building, the construction crew who brought the designs to life, and the local authorities who ensured compliance with building regulations. Acknowledging and understanding each stakeholder's role, expectations, and concerns was vital in fostering a collaborative and harmonious project environment.

Developing the Project Plan

The project timeline and milestones are the well-laid-out plan for our construction project. It outlines each task, assigns responsibilities, sets deliverables, and forecasts costs. For our commercial project, we developed a comprehensive project plan detailing every construction process aspect, from site preparation and foundation work to interior finishing and landscaping. This plan provided a roadmap for the project, guiding our day-to-day operations and serving as a reference point for tracking progress.

Estimating Project Costs

Just as a freight train conductor must balance the speed of the rail cars on the track to bring the load into port at a designated time, a project manager must balance the costs to create a financially viable project. Cost estimation for our commercial project involves a detailed analysis of each task. We considered the cost of labor, materials, equipment, permits, and overheads. This meticulous approach ensured our budget was realistic and comprehensive, reducing the likelihood of unexpected costs down the line.

Scheduling Project Activities

In the typically quick pace of construction, timing is everything. Scheduling project activities is like setting the tempo for our project from the ground up, ensuring each task starts and ends at the right time. We created a detailed schedule for our office building project that sequenced activities based on their dependencies. Using a Gantt chart, we visualized the timeline for each task, allowing us to coordinate resources effectively, anticipate bottlenecks, and keep the project on track.

As we dig deeper into commercial construction management, these planning strategies lay the foundation for effective execution and control. They equip us with the tools to navigate the complexities of commercial construction, enabling us to navigate our projects with precision and confidence. As we continue to explore, let's remember that in construction management, every detail counts, every plan matters, and every decision shapes the success of our project.

EXECUTION AND CONTROL PHASE

Coordinating with Subcontractors

On the grand scale of commercial construction, subcontractors play vital roles. They are the skilled tradespeople who bring their expertise to our construction site, performing specialized tasks from electrical installations to masonry work. Working with subcontractors is similar to managing a group of individuals, ensuring everyone does their part at the right time.

To execute our office building project, we needed multiple qualified subcontractors. Effective coordination with these teams required clear communication, precise scheduling, and efficient resource management. We held regular coordination meetings to discuss work progress, address concerns, and align all parties with the project objectives.

Implementing Quality Assurance Procedures

Quality in commercial construction is not just a goal; it's a commitment that permeates every phase of every task. Putting quality assurance procedures into action is like ensuring our tools are in top shape before starting a job. It provides that every step we take is precise and excellent.

For our office building project, we established a robust quality assurance system. It involved setting quality standards for each task, conducting regular inspections, and maintaining comprehensive documentation. This proactive approach helped us catch discrepancies early, minimizing rework and ensuring consistent quality across the project.

Tracking Project Performance

Keeping a pulse on the project's performance is integral to effective construction management. It's the heartbeat that tells us how our project is faring, indicating whether we're on track or need to adjust our course.

To track the performance of our commercial construction project, we used a combination of key performance indicators (KPIs), regular progress reports, and performance reviews. These tools provided real-time data on the project's cost, schedule, and quality performance, enabling us to make informed decisions and take timely corrective actions.

Managing Project Changes

Change is always part of construction projects. Effectively managing these changes is like adjusting our approach, ensuring we stay in sync with the evolving requirements.

During the execution of our office building project, we encountered several changes, from design modifications to revised regulatory requirements. We managed these changes using a formal change management process, which involved reviewing the proposed changes, assessing their impact, obtaining necessary approvals, and updating the project plan. This structured approach helped us maintain control over the project despite the shifting dynamics.

Ensuring Safety Standards

Safety is a paramount concern in any construction project. Ensuring the safety of all workers and stakeholders is like creating a protective bubble around our construction site, ensuring everyone gets to go home safe and healthy at the end of the day.

In our commercial construction project, we implemented stringent safety measures. These included regular safety training for workers, strict adherence to safety protocols, and routine safety audits. We also maintained a safety contingency plan to handle any potential emergencies. These measures ensured a safe and secure work environment, contributing to the project's success.

From coordinating with subcontractors and enforcing quality assurance procedures to tracking project performance, managing changes, and ensuring safety, the execution and control phase of our commercial construction project was a testament to the power of effective project management. It showcased how careful coordination, meticulous planning, and proactive management can turn the vision of a modern office building into a tangible reality. As we navigate the exciting world of construction management, these experiences provide valuable insights, shedding light on the practical aspects of managing a commercial construction project.

OVERCOMING CHALLENGES

Addressing Design Changes

In the fast-paced world of commercial construction, design changes can pop up like unforeseen elements in a well-laid-out construction plan. While our office building project was underway, the client decided to revise some aspects of the design, requesting an expansion of the lobby area and an upgrade in the HVAC system. Though beneficial for the end product, these alterations presented fresh challenges in terms of cost, material procurement, and rework.

We tackled these changes head-on, starting with analyzing the project timeline and budget implications. Revised blueprints were swiftly prepared, and the team was briefed about the modifications. By proactively managing these design changes, we prevented potential disruptions and kept the project on track.

Handling Budget Overruns

The delicate balance of a construction project budget can sometimes be burdened by unforeseen expenses, leading to budget overruns. Our office building project faced a similar challenge when material costs surged unexpectedly due to market fluctuations.

To manage this, we revisited our budget and looked for areas where we could optimize costs without compromising quality. We also negotiated with suppliers for possible price reductions and explored cost-effective alternative materials. This proactive approach helped us curb the budget overruns and maintain financial control over the project.

Resolving Labor Disputes

Cooperation amongst the workforce is a crucial element in the synchronization of construction. However, labor disputes can sometimes disrupt this harmony. During our project, a disagreement arose between two subcontracting teams over workspace boundaries, threatening to delay the project.

We facilitated a discussion between the two teams to resolve this issue, helping them voice their concerns and find a mutually agreeable solution. Additionally, we revisited our site management plan and made necessary adjustments to prevent similar disputes in the future. This prompt and empathetic response helped us maintain a positive work environment and ensure uninterrupted project progress.

Mitigating Weather-Related Delays

Construction, more often than not, starts with a plethora of exterior work, and weather can often play an unpredictable and disruptive role. Our project faced a significant delay when a few days of heavy rainfall made it impossible to proceed with the outdoor tasks.

To mitigate this challenge, we adjusted our project schedule, prioritizing indoor tasks that could be carried out despite the weather. We also used this time for equipment maintenance and staff training, ensuring productive use of the forced downtime. Once the weather cleared, we resumed the outdoor work with renewed vigor, making up for lost time.

Ensuring Compliance with Building Codes

Compliance with building codes and regulations is a non-negotiable aspect of any construction project. During the construction of our office building, new building regulations were introduced, necessitating modifications to our project.

We approached this challenge with a proactive and compliant mindset. We became familiar with the new regulations, assessed their implications for our project, and made the necessary adjustments in the design and construction processes. This adaptability ensured our project complied with the regulations, avoiding potential legal complications and penalties.

Tackling these diverse challenges, from design changes and budget overruns to labor disputes, weather-related delays, and building code compliance, brought valuable lessons in resilience, adaptability, and problem-solving. These experiences enriched our understanding of commercial construction management, teaching us the importance of preparedness, flexibility, and a proactive approach to overcoming hurdles and steering our projects toward success.

KEY TAKEAWAYS AND LESSONS LEARNED

Significance of Stakeholder Management

In our commercial construction project, we recognized that each stakeholder played a vital role, much like a medical team in a hospital. Ensuring all stakeholders were in tune with the project objectives was critical to maintaining collaboration, preventing disconnections between the key trades, and achieving the desired outcome.

We learned that effective stakeholder management involves identifying and understanding each stakeholder's role, expectations, and concerns. It fosters open communication, promotes collaboration, and ensures everyone feels valued and heard.

In practice, this meant holding regular meetings to update stakeholders about the project's progress, addressing their concerns promptly, and involving them in decision-making processes. This proactive approach helped build trust, enhance cooperation, and create a positive project environment.

Effective Leadership in Project Success

As we navigated the complex dynamics of commercial construction, the role of effective leadership emerged as an avenue toward success. Like a seasoned pilot flying a jetliner through a storm, a project manager's leadership skills are crucial in guiding a project through challenges and toward its objectives.

Our experience underscored that effective leadership is about managing tasks and inspiring and motivating the team. It's about setting a clear vision, fostering a positive work culture, and empowering team members to do their best.

In our project, we embodied this leadership approach by establishing clear goals, promoting open communication, and recognizing the contributions of our team members. This leadership style helped us cultivate a motivated, high-performing team driven to achieve project success.

Regular Performance Tracking

Just as over-the-road truck driver continually checks their map to ensure they're on the right course, we learned that regular performance tracking is essential to keep a construction project on track. It's about comparing the actual progress against the planned progress, identifying deviations, and taking corrective action.

We found that using key performance indicators (KPIs) and regular progress reports were practical tools for tracking project performance. These tools provided real-time data, enabling us to make informed decisions and adjust our course as needed.

For instance, when we noticed a delay in the framing phase of our project, we quickly identified the cause and took corrective action to get back on schedule. This proactive approach to performance tracking helped us maintain control over the project and steer it toward successful completion.

Value of Safety in Construction Management

In the often hazardous environment of a construction site, we learned that safety is not just a regulation; it's a commitment to protect our most valuable resource - our people. Ensuring the safety of all workers and stakeholders is paramount in managing a construction project.

In our commercial construction project, we implemented stringent safety measures, including regular safety training, strict adherence to safety protocols, and routine safety audits. We also maintained a safety contingency plan to handle potential emergencies.

These measures ensured a safe work environment and contributed to the project's success. They helped prevent accidents, reduce downtime, and enhance worker satisfaction. In essence, we learned that safety is not just about preventing harm; it's about fostering a culture of care and respect.

Every commercial construction project is a learning experience, offering valuable insights and lessons. As we reflect on these takeaways, we're reminded of the importance of stakeholder management, effective leadership, regular performance tracking, and safety in construction management. These principles are the cornerstones that support the edifice of a successful project. They guide us, inspire us, and help us to build not just structures but also a legacy of excellence and success.

As we prepare for our next project—an industrial construction job—we carry these lessons with us. They form the blueprint that guides us, the foundation that grounds us, and the machinery that propels us forward. So, let's roll up our sleeves and continue our exciting journey into the captivating field of construction project management.

9

NAVIGATING THE COMPLEXITIES OF INDUSTRIAL CONSTRUCTION MANAGEMENT

PICTURE THIS: a blended construction crew of multiple skilled trades is gearing up before starting a project. The tasks those trade workers perform that day slowly come together, forming a well-coordinated construction project. This is what planning an industrial construction should feel like. As the project manager, you are the leader, bringing order to the chaos, ensuring each element—each task, team, and resource—is in sync, performing its role flawlessly.

Industrial construction projects are like complex construction projects, intricate undertakings that demand a deep understanding of technical details, efficient allocation of resources, and a proactive approach to managing risks. In this chapter, we'll explore the world of industrial construction management and dive into a real-life case study that offers valuable insights and lessons.

PROJECT OVERVIEW AND PLANNING PHASE

Identifying Project Requirements

Our industrial project was a large-scale manufacturing plant. The first step, similar to defining the scope of a construction project, was to identify the project requirements. This involved detailed discussions with clients to understand their needs, operations, and expectations. We considered factors such as production capacity, machinery specifications, operational flow, environmental impact, and safety standards. Future expansion possibilities were also considered, ensuring the design and layout could accommodate growth.

Developing the Project Charter

With the project requirements clear, we developed the project charter. Much like a construction plan that outlines the details of a project, the project charter provides a high-level overview of the project. It outlined the project's objectives, scope, deliverables, milestones, and stakeholders. It also detailed the roles and responsibilities of the project team and set the lines of authority and communication. This document served as a reference point throughout the project, guiding decisions and ensuring alignment with the project's goals.

Creating the Risk Management Plan

In our construction analogy, the risk management plan is the safety net that catches any missteps, ensuring the project doesn't falter. For our industrial construction project, this involved identifying potential risks that could impact the project, from equipment failures and supply chain disruptions to regulatory changes and labor issues. We then assessed these risks based on their potential impact and likelihood of occurrence and developed strategies to mitigate or manage them. This proactive approach to risk management was crucial in navigating uncertainties and ensuring the project's success.

Establishing the Project Timeline

Much like a construction project's schedule, the project timeline sets the project's pace. It outlines when each task should start and finish, ensuring a smooth flow of activities. We developed a detailed project timeline that factored in the sequence and dependencies of tasks, allowing for sufficient buffer time to manage potential delays. This timeline, visualized through a Gantt chart, served as a roadmap for the project, guiding the team and helping us track progress effectively.

Determining Project Budget

Finally, just as a project manager ensures each aspect aligns with the project's goals, a project manager works to balance the budget. This involved estimating the costs of each task, from labor and materials to equipment, permits, and overheads. We used a combination of cost estimation techniques, including unit cost estimating and bottom-up estimating, to ensure a comprehensive and accurate budget. Regular tracking of actual expenses against the estimated budget was crucial to keep the project financially on track.

Much like the preparation before starting construction work, this planning phase sets the stage for a successful industrial construction project. It involved careful coordination, meticulous planning, and strategic decision-making. These efforts ensured a smooth start to our project, paving the way for a successful execution phase. As we explore the intricacies of industrial construction management, these planning strategies will serve as our guiding principles, leading us toward successful project completion.

EXECUTION AND CONTROL PHASE

Managing Project Crews

On an industrial construction project, diverse teams of professionals come together, each bringing their specialized skills to the table, yet all working towards a common goal. Although these workers bring their specific talents and job qualifications, they are all very seasoned in working closely together, often side-by-side on large industrial construction projects.

The role of the construction manager, similar to a construction crew leader, is to ensure all these different trades work and blend well together. From architects and engineers to construction workers and site supervisors, the construction manager must coordinate the efforts of various teams, aligning their tasks and timelines and fostering a collaborative and efficient working environment.

We used various strategies to manage our crews effectively in our industrial construction project. Regular crew meetings facilitated open communication, allowing us to discuss progress, address issues, and align everyone with the project objectives. Clear role definitions and performance metrics helped ensure accountability and motivate high performance.

Implementing Quality Management Systems

In a construction project, every task is crucial. A single error can impact the quality of the final structure. Implementing quality management systems is like ensuring each task is done to perfection. It involves setting quality standards for each task, monitoring work to ensure they are met, and taking corrective action when deviations occur.

We developed a robust quality management system for our project that included defined quality standards, regular quality inspections, and a comprehensive quality control and assurance plan. This proactive approach helped us maintain high quality across all tasks and deliver a final structure that met the client's expectations and industry standards.

Monitoring Project Milestones

In a construction project, the construction manager keeps track of the progress, ensuring each project phase is completed on time. Milestones are significant points in a project that represent the completion of critical phases or tasks. Monitoring these milestones helps track progress, identify delays, and take corrective action if needed.

In our industrial construction project, we used project management tools and regular progress reports to monitor our milestones.

Regular progress reviews helped us stay on schedule, make necessary adjustments, and inform our stakeholders about the project's status.

Handling Project Modifications

Just as a construction project may require adjustments in response to unexpected events, a construction project often requires modifications to handle unforeseen changes or issues. These could range from design alterations and scope changes to adjustments due to unforeseen site conditions or material availability.

Handling project modifications effectively requires flexibility, quick decision-making, and efficient communication. It's about assessing the impact of the change, exploring possible solutions, and implementing the most appropriate one.

In our industrial construction project, we encountered several modifications, from design changes due to updated regulations to adjustments in the construction process due to unexpected site conditions. We handled these modifications by promptly assessing their impact, discussing potential solutions with our team and stakeholders, and integrating the changes into our project plan.

Ensuring Environmental Compliance

A construction project doesn't just create a solid structure; it also respects the environment in which it operates. Similarly, an industrial construction project must deliver a functional and efficient design and minimize its environmental impact.

Ensuring environmental compliance involves understanding and adhering to environmental regulations, implementing sustainable construction practices, and monitoring environmental impact.

In our industrial construction project, environmental compliance was a top priority. We adhered to all relevant environmental regulations, implemented measures to minimize waste and pollution, and used sustainable materials wherever possible. Regular environmental audits ensured our compliance and helped us maintain our commitment to sustainability throughout the project.

CHALLENGES FACED AND OVERCOME

Managing Complex Technical Requirements

Industrial construction projects are designed as intricately as a complex machine, each part designed and assembled precisely to ensure flawless operation. The complexity of these projects lies not only in their scale but also in their technical requirements. These requirements span a broad spectrum for our manufacturing plant project, from installing specialized machinery and setting up complex electrical systems to creating efficient production lines and safe storage facilities.

The challenge was not just in understanding these technical requirements but also in translating them into practical construction solutions. This demanded a deep technical understanding, a keen eye for detail, and a problem-solving mindset. We met this challenge head-on, leveraging the expertise of our team, consulting with specialists, and collaborating closely with the client to ensure all technical requirements were met to the highest standards.

Dealing with High-Stake Risks

Every construction project carries risks, but these risks often come with higher stakes in industrial construction. The potential implications of risks such as equipment failure, structural faults, or safety incidents can be far-reaching, affecting not only the project but also the future operations of the facility.

In our project, we faced several high-stake risks, from potential delays in machinery delivery to challenges in installing complex systems. To manage these risks, we adopted a proactive and meticulous approach to risk management. We conducted thorough risk assessments, developed comprehensive mitigation plans, and maintained a strong focus on safety. This rigorous approach to risk management helped us navigate these high-stakes risks effectively and ensure the project's success.

Overcoming Supply Chain Issues

A construction project is only as strong as its weakest link, and in many cases, that link is the supply chain. Ensuring a steady supply of materials, equipment, and labor is crucial to keep the project on track. However, supply chain issues, such as delays in material delivery, equipment shortages, or labor unavailability, can disrupt the project's flow and cause significant delays.

In our industrial construction project, we experienced a few supply chain hiccups. However, instead of letting these issues derail our project, we tackled them proactively. We maintained strong relationships with multiple suppliers, allowing us to source alternatives when needed quickly. We also employed a flexible workforce strategy, enabling us to scale up or down based on our labor needs. These measures helped us overcome supply chain issues and maintain the project's momentum.

Navigating Stringent Regulatory Standards

Industrial construction projects often operate under a tight web of regulatory standards, covering aspects from environmental compliance and safety regulations to building codes and industry-specific guidelines. Navigating these stringent standards requires a thorough understanding of the regulations and their implications for the project.

For our project, we kept compliance at the forefront of our planning and execution processes. We familiarized ourselves with all relevant regulations, integrated compliance requirements into our project plan, and maintained regular communication with regulatory bodies. This proactive approach to compliance ensured our project adhered to all regulations and avoided potential legal complications.

High-Level Stakeholder Expectations

In an industrial construction project, the stakes are high, and so are the stakeholders' expectations. From the client expecting a functional and efficient facility to the workers expecting a safe and conducive work environment, managing these high-level stakeholder expectations is crucial.

In our project, we placed a high priority on stakeholder management. We maintained open communication channels with all stakeholders, informed them about the project's progress, and responded promptly to their concerns. We also strived to exceed their expectations wherever possible, delivering a project that met the functional requirements and incorporated elements of sustainability and innovation. This focus on stakeholder satisfaction was instrumental in earning us the trust and appreciation of all stakeholders, contributing significantly to the project's success.

Importance of Technical Expertise in Industrial Construction

Technical expertise is the cornerstone of industrial construction. The compass navigates the intricate maze of specifications, the torch that illuminates the path of complex installations, and the magic wand that transforms complex blueprints into tangible structures.

With our manufacturing plant project, the value of technical know-how became abundantly clear. This expertise allowed us to comprehend complex machinery requirements, calculate exacting tolerances, and ensure precise installations. We also leveraged our technical knowledge to solve unexpected problems, innovate solutions, and optimize processes. The technical prowess of our team was a crucial factor in the successful execution of the project, emphasizing the importance of fostering and utilizing technical expertise in industrial construction management.

Role of Comprehensive Risk Management

Risk management in industrial construction is like a well-choreographed ballet. It's a dance of anticipation and reaction, a balance of prevention and cure, and a performance that can distinguish between a project's success and failure.

In our manufacturing plant project, we observed firsthand the impact of comprehensive risk management. From anticipating potential equipment delivery delays and planning mitigation measures to reacting swiftly to unexpected site conditions and implementing corrective actions, we were constantly engaged in the dance of risk management. This proactive and comprehensive approach to managing risks was instrumental in keeping our project on track, underlining the significance of effective risk management in industrial construction.

Supply Chain Management

A robust supply chain is the lifeline of an industrial construction project. The steady rhythm of incoming materials and resources keeps the project moving, and reliability ensures the right resources are available at the right time.

During our project, we faced several supply chain challenges. However, we overcame these obstacles thanks to robust supply chain management strategies and maintained the project's momentum. We leveraged strong relationships with multiple suppliers, maintained a buffer stock of critical materials, and adopted a flexible workforce strategy to manage labor supply. These tactics helped us mitigate supply chain disruptions, underscoring the value of robust supply chain management in ensuring the smooth execution of industrial construction projects.

Benefits of Regulatory Compliance in Industrial Construction

Regulatory compliance in industrial construction is not just a legal requirement; it's a testament to the project's integrity, a commitment to safety, and a pledge to environmental responsibility.

We strived to ensure the highest regulatory compliance standards throughout our manufacturing plant project. We familiarized ourselves with all relevant regulations, integrated compliance requirements into our project plan, and maintained open communication with regulatory bodies. This commitment to compliance kept our project on the right side of State and Local regulations and enhanced its reputation and credibility. It served as a potent reminder of the significance of regulatory compliance in industrial construction management.

To recap what we've learned in this chapter, industrial construction management is a balance of coordination and collaboration, an exercise in anticipation and reaction, and a testament to the power of expertise, risk management, robust supply chain management, and regulatory compliance. These elements form the forward progress to which successful industrial construction projects ultimately deliver, creating a measured and successful industrial construction project filled with efficiency, reliability, and excellence.

Let's keep these insights with us as we move into the next chapter. They will guide our exploration of emerging trends in construction management, navigating us through the evolving landscape and construction innovations.

10

THE FUTURE OF CONSTRUCTION MANAGEMENT

A NEW ERA is beginning in the construction industry. Picture the excitement of a construction crew setting up a plethora of new technological scanning equipment, ready to head to a job site and make 3-D digital images of a large-scale construction project for the first time. That's the feeling as we stand on the edge of these exciting technological changes in construction management. We're regularly implementing efficient innovations that will reshape how we construct buildings.

This chapter dives into some of the most groundbreaking technological advancements transforming construction, including Building Information Modeling (BIM), drones, 3D printing, and augmented reality, to name a few. Just as a new piece of machinery brings efficiency to a construction site, these technologies reshape construction management, unlock new possibilities, and revolutionize our approach to building.

TECHNOLOGICAL ADVANCEMENTS IN CONSTRUCTION

Building Information Modeling (BIM)

Building Information Modeling, or BIM, is like the detailed digital blueprint for our construction project. It's a digital representation of a facility's physical and functional characteristics. It provides a shared knowledge resource for information about a facility and forms a reliable basis for decisions during its life cycle. BIM goes beyond traditional 2D plans by adding additional dimensions of time (4D), cost (5D), and even sustainability (6D) to the model.

Imagine visualizing the entire construction project, from design to demolition, in a single, interactive model. You can see how the building will look, how it will function, how much it will cost, and how long it will take to build, even before the first brick is laid. This allows for better project planning, improved stakeholder collaboration, and enhanced decision-making throughout the project lifecycle.

Drones and Robotics

Drones and robotics are like the skilled workers in our construction team, performing complex tasks with precision and efficiency. Drones, equipped with high-resolution cameras, can capture aerial images of a construction site, providing a bird's eye view of the progress. This can be particularly useful for large-scale projects, where manually inspecting the entire site could be time-consuming and potentially risky.

Alternatively, robots can automate repetitive, labor-intensive tasks, such as bricklaying, concrete pouring, or even welding. Not only does this save time and reduce labor costs, but it also improves the quality of work and reduces the risk of human error. It's like having a skilled worker who can perform the same task perfectly every time.

3D Printing in Construction

3D printing, or additive manufacturing, is like the advanced machinery in our construction team, turning ideas into reality. It involves creating a three-dimensional object from a digital model by adding material layer by layer. 3D printing can make building components, or even entire structures, with unprecedented speed and precision in construction.

Imagine being able to "print" a custom-designed house in just a few days or creating intricate architectural features at the click of a button. Not only does this dramatically speed up the construction process, but it also allows for greater design flexibility and reduces material waste.

Augmented and Virtual Reality

Augmented reality (AR) and virtual reality (VR) are like the guides in our construction team, providing a clear vision. AR overlaps digital information with the real world, while VR immerses the user in a completely virtual environment. In construction, AR can be used to visualize design plans on the actual site, while VR can be used to walk through a virtual building model, visually bringing to life what only exists in an idea or on paper.

Imagine seeing how a finished building will look on its site, even before construction begins, or walking through a virtual building model to inspect the layout and finishes. This improves design understanding and communication and allows for early detection and resolution of design conflicts.

Cloud-Based Construction Management Programs

Although cloud-driven CMPs (construction management programs) have been around in some form or another for over a decade, the makers of these programs have really come to understand the needs of the stakeholders, on-site construction managers, and even the skilled workers who are on a tight schedule. Additionally,

Construction management programs are the lifeline of a construction project, no matter whether it's a small residential house, a simple tenant improvement, a towering condominium building, or even an industrial manufacturing plant.

Construction management programs offer significant benefits and value by streamlining various aspects of construction projects. These platforms provide a centralized hub for project information, enabling seamless collaboration among team members, subcontractors, and stakeholders. With features like document management, project scheduling, and real-time communication tools, these programs enhance efficiency by reducing the risk of miscommunication and delays. The ability to automate routine tasks, such as document tracking and approval workflows, saves time and minimizes errors, contributing to improved project accuracy. Procore, a widely-used construction management software, highlights how its platform fosters collaboration and centralizes project data, promoting transparency and accountability throughout the project lifecycle.

Automation is a key strength of these programs, facilitating better resource allocation, cost control, and schedule adherence. For instance, scheduling tools help optimize project timelines, considering dependencies and resource availability. Moreover, advanced analytics capabilities within these systems can analyze historical project data to identify patterns and trends, allowing for predictive insights into potential issues. By proactively alerting project managers to potential risks and deviations, these programs empower teams to take corrective action before problems escalate. Autodesk BIM 360, a construction management platform utilizing Building Information Modeling (BIM), emphasizes its role in providing real-time insights and predicting project outcomes through data analytics.

Without a doubt, construction management programs automate mundane tasks and act as strategic tools that enhance overall project performance and mitigate risks.

Below is a list of the most widely used construction management programs and their features and benefits.

Procore: Procore is a leading cloud-based construction management software that offers a comprehensive suite of tools to streamline project management processes. With Procore, construction teams benefit from real-time collaboration, document management, and project tracking functionalities. The platform provides a centralized hub for project information, allowing teams to access and update data from anywhere, fostering enhanced communication and transparency. Procore's features include project scheduling, quality control, and budget management, contributing to improved efficiency and accuracy in construction projects. Additionally, its mobile capabilities empower field teams to access critical information on-site, reducing delays and improving decision-making. Procore enhances collaboration, automates project workflows, and delivers efficient project management solutions. (Reference: (Procore).

PlanGrid: PlanGrid is a construction productivity software focusing on real-time collaboration and document management for construction projects. With its user-friendly interface, PlanGrid allows teams to efficiently work on project plans and blueprints, reducing communication gaps. The platform enables teams to seamlessly access, share, and mark up project documents, improving project coordination and faster decision-making (Reference: PlanGrid).

Autodesk BIM 360: Autodesk BIM 360 is a comprehensive construction management platform that leverages Building Information Modeling (BIM) for enhanced collaboration and project delivery. It offers document management, design collaboration, and field management features to streamline workflows and improve project outcomes. BIM 360's cloud-based platform facilitates real-time data access, allowing teams to make informed decisions throughout the project lifecycle (Reference: Autodesk BIM 360).

Prolog: Prolog by Trimble is a robust project management solution that covers the entire project lifecycle, from preconstruction to project closeout. The software manages project information, facilitates collaboration, and ensures efficient data flow between project stakeholders. Prolog's features include document control, change management, and cost control, providing construction teams with the tools needed for effective project management (Reference: Trimble Prolog).

Viewpoint: Viewpoint offers a comprehensive construction management software solution integrating project management, accounting, and field operations. Viewpoint focuses on improving collaboration and project visibility, enabling construction companies to manage their projects more effectively. The platform's features include project financials, job costing, and document management, providing a centralized solution for construction project management (Reference: Viewpoint).

BuilderTREND: BuilderTREND is a cloud-based construction project management platform designed to streamline various aspects of construction projects. The software includes features for project scheduling, customer management, and document sharing. BuilderTREND's user-friendly interface and mobile capabilities empower construction teams to collaborate efficiently, enhancing overall project communication and coordination (Reference: BuilderTREND).

e-Builder: e-Builder is a construction program management solution focusing on controlling costs, managing documents, and facilitating collaboration for large construction projects. The platform offers features such as budget management, document control, and change order management to streamline project processes and enhance project visibility. e-Builder's emphasis on real-time collaboration contributes to improved efficiency in construction project management (Reference: e-Builder).

CMiC: CMiC provides an integrated construction management software solution covering project management, financials, and document management. The platform is designed to meet the unique needs of construction companies, offering features such as project controls, risk management, and resource management. CMiC's comprehensive approach aims to improve overall project performance and stakeholder collaboration (Reference: CMiC).

Sage 100 Contractor: Sage 100 Contractor is a construction project management and accounting solution designed for small to midsize construction businesses. The software offers project estimating, accounting, and service management features to streamline construction processes. Sage 100 Contractor focuses on improving project visibility and financial control, allowing construction companies to manage projects efficiently and make informed decisions. With modules for project management, payroll, and reporting, Sage 100 Contractor provides a comprehensive solution for the unique needs of construction businesses (Reference: Sage 100 Contractor).

Sage 300 Construction and Real Estate: Sage 300 Construction and Real Estate, formerly known as Timberline, is an integrated construction and property management solution for midsize to large construction companies. The platform covers project management, accounting, and procurement, offering project cost tracking, payroll, and financial reporting features. Sage 300 aims to provide construction companies with the tools needed for effective financial management and project control (Reference: Sage 300).

Internet of Things (IoT) in Construction

The Internet of Things (IoT) is like the communication network of our construction team, connecting all the elements to work in real-time. It involves connecting physical devices, like sensors and actuators, to the internet, allowing them to collect, share, and act on data.

In construction, IoT can monitor various aspects of a project in real-time, such as equipment usage, worker safety, or environmental conditions. Sensors placed on construction machinery can monitor use and performance, helping to schedule maintenance and prevent breakdowns. Wearable devices can monitor workers' health and safety, alerting supervisors to potential hazards. This real-time monitoring and data analysis can lead to more informed decision-making, improved efficiency, and enhanced security on the construction site.

As we embrace these technological advancements, the future of construction management looks promising. The construction process is evolving, with new tools like BIM, drones, robotics, 3D printing, AR, VR, and IoT contributing to the efficiency and innovation of our work. As we continue to explore and adopt these technologies, we're not just constructing buildings but building the future.

GREEN BUILDING AND SUSTAINABILITY

Energy-Efficient Construction Methods

Energy efficiency in construction is similar to that of major automobile manufacturers professing their dedication to increasing their EV (electric vehicle) output in the coming decades. The focus is on constructing buildings that consume less energy, thus reducing their carbon footprint and promoting sustainability. This can be achieved through various methods, such as using high-performance windows and insulation, installing energy-efficient lighting and HVAC systems, and incorporating renewable energy sources like solar or wind power.

Imagine a building not just anchored to the earth but working with it, harnessing the sun's light to power its lights or the earth's heat to warm its rooms. That's the magic of energy-efficient construction, a magic that's transforming the construction industry and paving the way for a greener, more sustainable future.

Recycled and Sustainable Materials

In the always-evolving facets of sustainable construction, recycled, repurposed, and sustainable materials play a crucial role. The useability or the re-useability of materials harvested from buildings being demolished or new materials created from old recycled materials is the way of the future of construction. Preserving as many items as possible from a building slated for destruction saves the environmental aspect of producing brand-new materials. It reiterates the sustainability factor, which is front and center in today's construction projects. These materials, which are either derived from sustainable sources or recycled from waste products, reduce the environmental impact of construction.

From buildings made of recycled steel or reclaimed wood to bricks made from fly ash or plastic waste, the possibilities are as diverse as they are innovative. By using recycled and sustainable materials, we're not just building structures; we're also building a better, more sustainable world.

Water Conservation Techniques

Water, the essence of life, is a critical resource that needs to be conserved. In green construction, water conservation techniques are the design factor that syncs our projects with the ebb and flow of nature's resources. These techniques reduce water usage and promote efficient use in construction projects.

Techniques like rainwater harvesting, greywater recycling, and water-efficient fixtures can significantly reduce a building's water footprint. Imagine a facility that collects the rain from the skies for its water needs or reuses its greywater to nourish its green spaces. That's the power of water conservation in green construction.

Green Building Certifications

Just as a concert earns applause for its performance, green buildings earn certifications for their environmental performance. Green building certifications, like LEED (Leadership in Energy and Environmental Design) or BREEAM (Building Research Establishment Environmental Assessment Method), provide a standard for measuring the sustainability of buildings.

These certifications consider various aspects of sustainability, including energy efficiency, water conservation, use of sustainable materials, and indoor environmental quality. Achieving a green building certification is not just about gaining recognition; it's about striving for excellence in sustainability, pushing boundaries, and setting new standards in green construction.

Climate Change and Construction

Some methods of construction, stretching back decades, are being rewritten by the winds of change, specifically climate change. Rising global temperatures, increasing instances of extreme weather events, and rising sea levels are prompting the industry to rethink traditional construction practices.

In response to these challenges, adaptive construction methods are being developed. These include designing buildings to withstand extreme weather events, using materials that can withstand higher temperatures, and elevating buildings in coastal areas to protect against sea-level rise. The impact of climate change is shaping our construction practices and emphasizing the importance of green and sustainable construction in creating a resilient future.

THE IMPACT OF GLOBALIZATION ON CONSTRUCTION MANAGEMENT

Cross-Border Construction Projects

Globalization has expanded the need for additional skills that a construction project manager may need to have in their toolkit, enabling us to perform globally. Construction projects are increasingly crossing borders, no longer confined to local or national boundaries, creating a new genre of cross-border construction projects.

Imagine constructing a high-speed rail network that connects two countries or building a multinational corporation's headquarters in a foreign land. These projects bring unique opportunities, from tapping into new markets to gaining international exposure. However, they also pose challenges, such as dealing with different regulatory environments, navigating foreign business cultures, and managing logistics over long distances.

These cross-border projects require construction managers to adapt to an international context, understand and respect cultural differences, comply with foreign regulations, and coordinate resources across borders. It's like giving a presentation on global LEED-building efforts within different countries; each country brings its unique style, and all countries come together to create a collective standardized model.

International Standards and Regulations

The international construction world is governed by a complex web of standards and regulations; each standard is written to ensure the construction technique is safe, quality-assured, and synchronizes with the all-encompassing regulations for individual construction projects. As construction projects cross borders, they encounter different standards and regulations, making the final completion of a project even more complex.

For instance, the safety regulations that apply to a construction project in the United States may differ from those in the European Union. A building designed for Canada may not meet the seismic resistance standards required in Japan.

Adhering to these international construction standards and regulations is crucial to ensure cross-border construction projects' safety, functionality, and sustainability.

Global Economic Trends on Construction

The influence of the global economy plays a significant role in shaping the landscape of the construction industry. Economic growth fuels construction activity, while economic downturns can slow it down. Global economic trends, such as fluctuations in commodity prices, exchange rates, or interest rates, can significantly impact construction projects, particularly those across borders.

For instance, a rise in steel prices on the global market can inflate the budgets of construction projects worldwide. Strengthening the local currency against the dollar can make imported construction materials more expensive. Staying attentive to these global economic trends and understanding their potential impact on the project is crucial for construction managers in the globalized world.

Multicultural Workforce Management

Our global construction landscape comprises diverse professionals, each bringing unique skills, perspectives, and cultural backgrounds to the project. This diversity enriches our learning and calls for a nuanced approach to workforce management.

Construction managers must respect and value cultural differences in a multicultural workforce, promote inclusivity, and ensure clear and effective communication. For instance, language barriers can be overcome through translation services or bilingual staff. Cultural sensitivities can be addressed through diversity training and inclusive policies.

By appreciating the unique knowledge base and set of skills each member brings to our project, we can create a construction job site that's rich, diverse, and truly global.

THE ROLE OF GOVERNMENT REGULATIONS AND POLICIES

Occupational Safety and Health Regulations

Safety is the common denominator on every construction job site across the globe. It protects the workforce from harm and allows everyone to return to their family at the end of every workday.

Government regulations, such as those set forth by the Occupational Safety and Health Administration (OSHA), serve as the rulebook of sorts. These regulations stipulate safety standards that construction projects must adhere to, from using personal protective equipment to implementing safe operating procedures. They're the life-saving measures that ensure the commotion of a construction site doesn't descend into chaos, protecting workers from potential hazards and promoting a safety culture.

Building Codes and Standards

The construction industry is well-versed in complying with various building codes and standards. These regulations, set by local, national, or international bodies, dictate the minimum requirements for constructing safe and functional buildings. They're the architectural equivalent of a set of written instructions guiding the construction process from design to completion. Consider a building code as the finished product from these instructions, setting the rules for aspects like structural integrity, fire resistance, and accessibility. Adherence to these building codes and standards safeguards the occupants' well-being and ensures the building can sustain its integrity over time.

Environmental Regulations

Like any significant human activity, construction projects affect the environment. Government environmental regulations serve as the ecological conscience of the construction industry, guiding its interactions with nature. These regulations cover various considerations, from managing waste and reducing emissions to protecting local habitats. Adherence to these regulations ensures that the construction projects contribute to a sustainable future, creating structures that coexist harmoniously with nature.

Impact of Government Infrastructure Spending

By investing in infrastructure projects, governments can stimulate economic growth, create jobs, and enhance the quality of life. This investment can range from public housing and road networks to schools and healthcare facilities. Government infrastructure spending increases the probability of our construction projects, defining potential projects' scale, scope, and timing. It significantly shapes the industry's landscape, influences construction demand, and drives innovation.

In the grand scope of construction management, government regulations and policies guide the industry toward safety, sustainability, and prosperity. These regulations set the tone and the expectations for many construction projects, ensuring the construction industry plays its part in building a safer, greener, and more prosperous world.

As we wrap up this book, which has hopefully given you a close-up understanding of construction project management, I want to give you a boost of confidence and excitement for what lies ahead. The construction world is always changing, and armed with the insights you've gained here, you're set to tackle the challenges and the benefits that go hand in hand in a construction project management career.

Whether you're a pro who read this book to refine your skills or someone completely new to construction management, remember that every project is a chance for you to learn and become a better construction manager. Use the collaborative tools you've learned in this book, like those that streamline communication and document handling, and watch how your projects will sometimes seem effortless. The future of construction is always evolving, and I know your hard work, combined with the tools you now have at your disposal, will lead to successful projects.

So, as you step out into the construction world, think about the wisdom shared in this book. Technology can be your digital partner in your career, helping you work smarter and even predict potential challenges. Automating tasks isn't just convenient; it's a smart move in this fast-paced industry. Like building a solid structure, your skills and knowledge are the foundation of your success. Whether you're out on the site or planning strategically, your journey in construction is a testament to your dedication.

Here's to the exciting projects waiting for you, the lessons you'll pick up along the way, and the impact you'll make in the construction scene. Cheers to your success!

11

GLOSSARY

As THIS BOOK is written primarily for those looking to gain insights into the construction industry and learn about becoming a construction project manager, we thought it would be beneficial to provide a glossary of many terms used in this book and additional terms you might find helpful while doing further research into the construction management field.

This list of glossary terms is in no way meant to be an exhaustive list. This list is compiled from a subset of the most commonly used terms in construction and construction project management.

A

ADA (Americans with Disabilities Act): A U.S. law that prohibits discrimination based on disability, ensuring accessibility and accommodations in various areas, including construction.

Addendum: A document issued to provide additional information, clarification, or modifications to the original construction documents or contracts.

Aggregate: Crushed stone, gravel, or sand used in construction.

Agile Project Management: A project management approach emphasizing flexibility, collaboration, and adaptability to respond to changing project requirements throughout construction.

All-In Rate: The total cost per unit of work, including direct and indirect fees, overhead, and profit margins.

Alterations: Changes or modifications made to an existing building or structure, often involving renovations, remodels, or adjustments to the original design.

Alternate Bid: A bid submitted for a construction project that offers an alternative solution or approach, often with different materials or methods, providing flexibility in project selection.

Anchor Bolt: An anchor bolt is a heavy-duty bolt designed to attach objects or structures to concrete securely. Typically used in construction, these bolts are embedded into the concrete during its pouring, providing a stable and anchored connection.

Apparent Low Bidder: The contractor who submits the lowest bid for a construction project based on initial review before further evaluation and confirmation.

Application for Payment: A formal request submitted by a contractor to the project owner or client for payment detailing the work completed and associated costs during a specific billing period.

Approved Bidders List: A list of contractors or construction firms that have been evaluated and approved to participate in the bidding process for a specific project.

Approved Changes: Modifications or adjustments to the original construction plans that have been reviewed and accepted by the project owner, architect, or relevant authorities.

Arch: An arch is a curved structural element that spans an opening, supporting the weight above it. Arches have been used in architecture for centuries for their ability to distribute loads and provide strength and stability.

Architect of Record: The architect responsible for the overall design and coordination of a construction project, often the lead architect overseeing the project's construction phase.

As-Built Drawings: Final revision drawings that reflect the actual construction of a project, incorporating changes made during the building process.

Asphalt: Asphalt refers to a black, sticky, and highly viscous liquid or semi-solid form of petroleum. In construction, it commonly refers to asphalt concrete, a composite material used for road construction. It consists of asphalt binder and mineral aggregate.

Auger: A drilling device or tool with a helical screw blade that rotates to create a hole in a material, typically soil or wood. Augers are commonly used in construction for digging holes for foundations, fence posts, or other applications.

B

Backfill: The process of refilling an excavated area with soil or other material to restore the ground to its original level or provide support to structures

Beam: A horizontal structural member that carries vertical loads, typically supported by columns or walls. Beams are crucial for distributing the weight of a structure and supporting the floors or roof.

Bid: A formal proposal submitted by a contractor or construction firm outlining the cost and details of the work they are willing to undertake for a construction project.

Bid Bond: A financial guarantee a contractor provides with their bid, assuring the project owner that they will enter into a contract if awarded the project.

Bid Documents: The collection of documents, including plans, specifications, and contract terms, provided to prospective bidders for their use in preparing bids for a construction project.

Bidding Division: The section or segment of a construction project open for competitive bidding, often specifying a particular scope of work. Each trade-specific discipline is assigned a division number. For example - Plumbing: Division 22. Mechanical/HVAC: Division 23. Electrical: Division 26.

Bill of Quantities (BOQ): A detailed document specifying the quantities and types of materials, labor, and services required for a construction project for cost estimation and bidding.

Blocking: Blocking refers to tasks that cannot be worked on or "blocked" from someone starting work until a previous task or subtask is complete. This prevents a broken workflow when dependencies are set to block someone from moving forward with the project.

Blueprint (construction): Two-dimensional drawings that contain the details needed for a construction project. These details are required to request permits, determine the construction schedule, and eventually do the construction itself.

Bond: A financial guarantee, which can take the form of a bid bond, performance bond, or payment bond, ensuring fulfillment of contractual obligations and financial protection for the project owner.

Bottleneck: A point in a construction process where the workflow is slowed or obstructed, often causing delays in the project timeline.

Brick: A rectangular block made of fired clay or concrete, commonly used as a building material in construction for walls, facades, and other structural elements.

Building Code: A set of regulations specifying standards for the construction and safety of buildings.

Building Envelope: The physical barrier or shell of a building that separates the interior from the exterior environment, including walls, roof, windows, and doors.

Building Inspector/Official: A professional responsible for inspecting construction projects to ensure compliance with building codes, zoning regulations, and safety standards.

Building Permit: A formal authorization issued by the local government or building department allowing the construction or modification of a building or structure in compliance with regulations.

Budget: The estimated financial plan for a construction project detailing expected costs and allocations

C

Caisson: A Caisson is a foundation used in deep water or soft soil. The base provides a stable foundation filled with concrete for structures built on top of it. Bridges, docks, and large structures often use caisson construction (see Piles).

Caulk: A material, often a flexible sealant, used to fill gaps or joints in construction to prevent air, water, or dust infiltration. Caulk is applied to create a watertight or airtight seal.

Change Order: A document that modifies the original construction contract, detailing changes in project scope, time, or cost.

Certificate of Occupancy (COI):

Claim: A formal request or demand by one party in a construction project for adjustments or compensation due to unforeseen circumstances, changes, or disputes.

Codes: Building codes or regulations set by local authorities or jurisdictions that dictate the minimum standards for construction, ensuring safety, health, and structural integrity.

Collaboration: The cooperative effort of various construction team members, including architects, contractors, and subcontractors, to achieve project goals.

Column: A vertical structural element that supports loads from above, typically consisting of a cylindrical or square-shaped shaft and a base. Columns are essential for providing vertical support to structures.

Commissioning: The process of ensuring that building systems and components are installed, tested, and function according to the design and operational requirements.

Concrete: A versatile construction material composed of cement, aggregates (sand and gravel), and water. It forms a durable and strong substance used in various construction applications when mixed.

Constructability: The extent to which a construction project can be successfully and efficiently built, considering design, logistics, and available resources.

Construction Coordination: Managing and synchronizing various construction activities, schedules, and resources to ensure a smooth and efficient project workflow.

Construction Management Software: Digital tools and platforms designed to streamline and enhance construction project management, including scheduling, budgeting, and communication.

Construction Manager (CM): A professional hired to oversee and manage various aspects of a construction project, including planning, coordination, and ensuring adherence to project goals.

Contingency: An allowance for unexpected costs or changes in a construction project, often set aside to address unforeseen events or uncertainties.

Contractability: The degree to which a construction project's scope, requirements, and specifications can be clearly defined and included in a contractual agreement.

Contractor: Individual or company responsible for executing construction work.

Cost Breakdown: A detailed analysis of the various components and items contributing to the overall cost of a construction project, providing transparency and clarity.

Cost Plus Contract: A construction contract where the contractor is reimbursed for the costs incurred during construction, plus an additional agreed-upon percentage or fee.

Crane: A large machine equipped with a hoist, wire ropes, or chains to lift and move heavy materials during construction. Cranes are essential for placing steel beams, concrete elements, or other large components.

Critical Path Method (CPM): A project management technique that identifies the sequence of activities with the most extended duration, determining the minimum time required to complete a construction project.

D

Daily Construction Report: A document prepared by the construction team that summarizes daily activities, progress, issues, and other relevant information on a construction site.

Date of Substantial Completion: When a construction project, or a designated phase, has reached a point where the work is considered substantially complete, allowing the owner to use or occupy the space.

Defects Liability Period: The period after project completion during which the contractor is responsible for rectifying defects at no extra cost.

Demising Walls: Walls that separate different occupancies or tenancies within a building, often used in multi-tenant structures to define individual spaces.

Demolition: The intentional destruction or dismantling of structures or buildings, often to make way for new construction or redevelopment.

Dependencies: The relationships between different tasks or activities in a construction project, where one task's completion may depend on another's completion.

Design-Build: A project delivery method where a single entity, typically a design-build firm, is responsible for both the design and construction of a project, streamlining communication and project management.

Door Jamb: The vertical or horizontal framing components surrounding a door opening, consisting of the side jambs and head jamb. It provides support and a frame for the door.

Drawings: Graphic representations or plans that illustrate the design and details of a construction project.

Drainage: The system or process of directing and controlling water flow away from a construction site, building, or structure to prevent water damage and erosion.

Dry Mix: A construction material, such as mortar or concrete mix, that is pre-packaged and does not require additional water on-site. It is often used for convenience and consistency.

E

Earned Value Management (EVM): A project management technique that tracks the progress and performance of a project.

Earthquake-resistant: Design or construction practices that minimize damage and ensure structural integrity during an earthquake. Techniques include using flexible materials and reinforcing structures to withstand seismic forces.

Electrical Wiring: The conductors, cables, and devices transmit electrical power and signals within a building. It includes wiring for lighting, outlets, switches, and other electrical components.

Elevation: A scaled drawing or plan that shows the vertical arrangement of a building or structure, indicating the height and location of walls, openings, and other features.

Estimate: A calculation of the expected cost of a construction project based on available information.

Excavation: Digging or removing earth to prepare a construction site.

Excavator: A heavy construction machine with a bucket, shovel, or scoop attachment used for digging and moving earth, debris, or other materials during excavation or earthmoving projects.

F

Fast-Track: A project delivery method that overlaps design and construction phases to expedite project completion.

Feasibility Phase: The initial stage of a construction project where a comprehensive analysis is conducted to assess the viability, costs, risks, and potential outcomes before committing to full-scale development.

Field Construction Manager: A professional overseeing and managing on-site construction activities, ensuring adherence to plans, timelines, and quality standards.

Field Work Order (Field Order): A document issued during construction to authorize changes or adjustments to the project that were not included in the original contract, often used for minor modifications.

Final Completion: The point in a construction project where all work has been completed, inspected, and approved, and the project is ready for occupancy or use according to the project requirements.

Final Inspection: An inspection conducted to ensure that a construction project meets all requirements before completion.

Flashing: Metal or waterproof material installed at joints, intersections, or transitions in a building to prevent water penetration. Flashing directs water away from vulnerable areas, such as roof valleys or around windows.

Follow-Up: The process of checking and ensuring that previous construction tasks or actions have been completed according to specifications.

Foundation: The substructure of a building that supports and distributes its load to the ground. Depending on soil conditions, foundations can be shallow (slab-on-grade) or deep (piles or caissons).

Framing: The structural framework of a building, including the vertical studs, horizontal beams, and other components that support the floors, walls, and roof.

G

Gantt Chart: A visual representation of a project schedule that uses bars or lines to illustrate various elements or tasks' start and finish dates, providing a timeline view of project activities.

General Conditions: The portion of a construction contract that outlines the general requirements, terms, and conditions applicable to the entire project, including administrative and procedural aspects.

General Contractor: The primary contractor overseeing and managing the entire construction project, including coordinating subcontractors, managing schedules, and ensuring overall project success.

Geotechnical Engineering: The branch of civil engineering that deals with the behavior of earth materials, such as soil and rock, in relation to construction projects.

Gravel: Small, loose rock particles are often used as a base material for construction projects such as roads, driveways, and foundations due to their ability to provide drainage and support.

Green Building: Construction practices that prioritize environmental sustainability and resource efficiency.

Grout: A mixture of cement, water, sand, or other fine aggregates that fill gaps or spaces between tiles, blocks, or structural elements, providing stability and support.

Guardrail: A protective barrier or railing installed along the edges of platforms, balconies, or elevated surfaces to prevent falls and enhance safety.

Gypsum: A mineral used in construction to produce gypsum board (drywall), a widely used material for interior wall finishes and ceilings.

H

Hammer: A handheld tool with a heavy metal head, typically used for driving nails into wood or other materials. It is a fundamental tool in construction and carpentry.

Handrail: A horizontal or sloping rail that provides support and guidance for individuals ascending or descending stairs, ramps, or other elevated surfaces.

Hard Costs: Direct construction costs, including materials, labor, and equipment.

Hard Hat: A safety helmet that protects the head from falling objects or impacts on construction sites. It is a standard personal protective equipment (PPE) for construction workers.

Homeowner's Association (HOA): An organization in a residential community that enforces rules and regulations regarding property use and appearance.

HVAC: Abbreviation for Heating, Ventilation, and Air Conditioning systems. HVAC systems control buildings' temperature, humidity, and air quality to provide a comfortable and healthy environment.

I

I-beam: A structural steel beam with an "I" shape, commonly used to support floors and roofs in buildings.

Infill Development: The process of developing vacant or underused parcels of land within existing urban areas.

Independent Contractor: A self-employed individual or entity hired by another party to perform a specific task or provide a service. Independent contractors are not considered employees and are responsible for their taxes and benefits.

Inspection: Examination of construction work to ensure it complies with building codes and project specifications.

Insulation: Material used to reduce heat transfer or sound transmission between different areas within a building.

IRFP/RFP (Invitation/Request for Proposal): IRFP is an Invitation for Request for Proposal, and RFP is a Request for Proposal. Both terms refer to a document or announcement inviting qualified individuals or companies to submit proposals for a specific project or service. The document typically outlines the project requirements, criteria for selection, and submission instructions.

Ironworker: A skilled tradesperson who specializes in working with structural iron and steel for construction projects.

Irrigation: The artificial application of water to soil or land to assist in the growth of plants.

Issue (context blueprints): To release or distribute documents, such as plans or changes, to relevant parties involved in the construction project.

Issue Log: A record that tracks and documents issues, challenges, or discrepancies identified during construction.

Issue Management: The systematic process of identifying, assessing, and resolving logged problems or challenges that arise during the construction project.

Issue Tracking: The ongoing monitoring and documentation of logged issues throughout the construction project life cycle.

Issue Types: Categories or classifications of logged construction issues, such as design discrepancies, material defects, or scheduling conflicts.

J

Jack Stud: A vertical framing member that supports the header in a framed opening, providing additional support.

Job Order Contracting (JOC): A construction procurement method where contractors are pre-selected, and projects are awarded based on unit prices.

Joint Compound: Plaster-like material that covers joints and seams in drywall installations for a smooth surface.

Joint Venture: A business arrangement where two or more parties collaborate to undertake a specific construction project.

Joist Hanger: Metal bracket designed to support the end of a joist and attach it to another structural element.

Junction Box: An enclosure that protects electrical connections, wires, and cables.

K

Key Performance Indicator (KPI): Quantifiable metrics used to evaluate the success and performance of a construction project.

Kickoff Meeting: An initial meeting at the start of a construction project to outline goals, roles, responsibilities, and expectations among project stakeholders.

Kicker: Short, inclined framing member used to provide additional support or alignment, often used in forms for concrete placement.

Kickplate: A protective metal plate is installed at the bottom of doors or walls to prevent damage from kicks or impacts.

Kilowatt-Hour (kWh): A unit of energy measurement commonly used in construction for electricity consumption.

Knee Wall: Short wall, typically found in attics or under sloped roofs, positioned between the floor and the roof rafters.

Knockdown Texture: Textured finish applied to walls or ceilings, created by spraying joint compound and then lightly knocking it down with a trowel.

L

Lally Column: A vertical structural support column, often filled with concrete, provides additional support for beams or girders in a building.

Laminate Flooring: A type of flooring that simulates the appearance of hardwood or stone by using a photographic layer under a protective transparent layer.

Lath: A material consisting of narrow strips of wood or metal used as a base for plaster or stucco on walls or ceilings.

Letter of Intent: A document expressing the intention of one party to engage in a particular business arrangement or transaction with another party. It outlines the key terms and conditions and is often a preliminary step before formalizing a contract.

Level: A tool to determine a surface's horizontal or vertical orientation, ensuring it is perfectly flat or plumb.

LEED: Acronym for Leadership in Energy and Environmental Design, a green building certification program that recognizes sustainable construction practices.

Lien (Mechanics or Material): A legal claim against a property as security for the payment of a debt or the performance of an obligation. In construction, contractors or suppliers often use mechanics and material liens to secure compensation for labor or materials provided.

Lien Release: A document executed by the party holding a lien (e.g., a contractor or supplier) to release the claimed interest in a property once payment has been received.

Lien Waiver: A document signed by a party with a potential mechanics or material lien claim, relinquishing their right to file a lien against a property. This is often done upon receiving payment for services or materials.

Long-Lead: Refers to items or materials in a construction project that have a longer production or delivery time and thus require early planning and procurement to avoid delays in the overall project schedule.

M

Master Schedule: An overarching and comprehensive schedule that outlines the timelines and sequencing of all activities and tasks in a construction project. It provides a high-level overview of the entire project timeline.

Meeting Agenda: A structured document outlining a construction project meeting's topics, discussions, and objectives.

Meeting Minutes: A written record summarizing discussions, decisions, and actions during construction project meetings.

Milestones: Significant events or achievements in a construction project, often used to track progress and assess adherence to the project timeline.

Millwork: Custom-made woodwork or cabinetry produced in a mill, including doors, window casings, and other architectural elements.

Mortar: A mixture of cement, sand, and water used as a bonding agent in masonry to hold bricks or stones together.

Mullion: A vertical or horizontal element that divides and supports the panes of a window or the panels of a door.

Masonry: The construction or craft of building with bricks, stones, or concrete blocks, often using mortar to bind them together.

N

Nailer (Nail Gun): An electric, battery, or air-powered tool used to drive nails into wood or other materials, commonly employed in framing or carpentry.

Non-load-bearing Wall: A wall that does not support the structure above it and is not essential for the stability of the building.

Notch: A V-shaped cut or groove made in a material, often used in carpentry or construction for fitting pieces together.

Notice of Award: A formal communication from a project owner or client to the selected contractor, officially notifying them that their bid has been accepted and they have been awarded the contract for the project.

Notice to Proceed: A formal written communication from the project owner or client to the contractor authorizing them to commence work on the project. It indicates that all necessary contractual requirements have been met, and the project can begin.

O

Occupancy Phase: The stage in a construction project where the completed structure is ready for use, occupation, or operation. It involves final inspections, approvals, and the transition to the facility's intended use.

Occupational Safety and Health Administration (OSHA): The federal agency that's part of the U.S. Department of Labor. OSHA's mission is to protect worker health and safety.

On-site Supervision: The presence and oversight of a construction professional, often a project manager or site supervisor, on the construction site to ensure that work is progressing according to plans, specifications, and safety standards.

Overhang: The extension of a roof or floor beyond the external walls of a building, providing shade or protection from the elements.

OSHA Regulations: the Occupational Safety and Health Administration (OSHA) sets guidelines and standards to ensure safe and healthy working conditions.

Outlet: A device or receptacle on a wall or panel that provides access to electrical power for devices and appliances.

P

Paver: A flat, usually square or rectangular, piece of stone, concrete, or other material used for paving surfaces like driveways, walkways, or patios.

Performance Bond: A financial guarantee provided by a contractor to the project owner, ensuring that the contracted work will be completed according to the terms of the contract. It protects the owner in case of non-performance by the contractor.

Phased Construction: A construction approach where the project is divided into distinct phases, allowing for partial completion and use of certain portions before the entire project is finished.

Piles: Piles are long cylinders made of solid material, such as concrete. Piles are pushed into the ground to act as a steady support for structures built on top of them. Piles transfer the loads from structures to hard strata, rocks, or soil with high bearing capacity.

Plaster: A construction material composed of gypsum, lime, or cement mixed with sand and water, applied in a paste-like form to walls and ceilings for a smooth finish.

Plumbing: The system of pipes, fixtures, and other apparatuses used to distribute water, gas, or sewage within a building or structure.

Pneumatic Drill: A drill powered by compressed air, commonly used in construction for drilling holes in various materials.

Preconstruction Phase: The initial stage of a construction project involves planning, design development, budgeting, and other preparatory activities before actual construction begins.

Preliminary Lien Notice: A notice provided by a contractor or supplier to alert the property owner and other relevant parties that they have provided or will be providing labor or materials to the construction project.

Pre-qualification: The process of assessing and evaluating the capabilities, qualifications, and financial stability of contractors or subcontractors before inviting them to bid on a construction project.

Private Sector: The segment of the economy that consists of private individuals and businesses, as opposed to the public sector. In construction, private sector projects are typically initiated and funded by private entities.

Product Data: Information provided by manufacturers or suppliers about the characteristics, specifications, and performance of construction materials or products.

Progress Payment: Payments made to a contractor at predetermined stages of project completion based on the percentage of work completed or specific milestones achieved.

Project Budget: The total allocated funds for a construction project, including costs for materials, labor, equipment, and overhead.

Project Directory: A document or system that contains contact information for key individuals and entities involved in a construction project, facilitating communication and coordination.

Project Manager: The individual responsible for planning, organizing, and overseeing all aspects of a construction project, ensuring it is completed on time and within budget.

Project Plan: A comprehensive document outlining the goals, tasks, timelines, and resources required for the successful completion of a construction project.

Project Portfolio Management (PPM): The centralized management and coordination of multiple construction projects within an organization to optimize resources and achieve strategic goals.

Project Stakeholder: Individuals or groups interested in or affected by the outcome of a construction project, including owners, contractors, subcontractors, and regulatory authorities.

Project Timeline: A visual representation of a construction project's chronological sequence of tasks and milestones, illustrating the planned duration.

Proposal: A formal document submitted by a contractor or consultant in response to a request for proposals (RFP) outlining their approach, qualifications, and cost for a specific project.

Proposal Form: A standardized document for submitting proposals, typically outlining critical information such as scope of work, pricing, and terms and conditions.

Public Sector: The segment of the economy that involves government entities and publicly funded projects. Public sector construction projects are initiated and financed by government agencies.

Punch List: A list of minor tasks, corrections, or finishing touches that must be completed before a construction project is complete and ready for occupancy or use.

Purchase Order: A formal document issued by a buyer to a seller indicating the types, quantities, and agreed-upon prices for products or services to be delivered.

Q

Quality Assurance: The systematic process of ensuring that construction work meets specified quality standards and adheres to regulations and requirements.

Quality Management Plan: A document outlining the processes, procedures, and criteria for maintaining and achieving quality in construction projects.

Quality Planning: Defining quality standards, specifications, and methods to be used in a construction project.

Quarry: A place where natural stone, rock, or minerals are extracted from the earth for use in construction.

Quarter Round: A trim molding with a cross-sectional quarter-circle shape, often used to cover gaps between flooring and baseboards.

Quoins: Large, usually rectangular, blocks of stone or other material used at the corners of a building to provide structural support and visual emphasis.

QuietRock: A brand of sound-dampening drywall designed to reduce sound transmission between rooms or areas.

R

Rafter: A sloping beam that supports the roof and extends from the top of the wall to the ridge or hip.

Rebar: Short for reinforcing bar, it is a steel bar or mesh used to reinforce concrete and masonry structures.

Record Drawings: Also known as as-built drawings, the final drawings reflect any changes made during construction. They document the actual, as-constructed conditions of the project.

Release of Lien: A document issued by a contractor, subcontractor, or supplier to release their claim or lien on a property. It confirms that payment has been received, and they waive their right to file a lien against the property.

Resource Allocation: The strategic assignment of resources, including labor, materials, and equipment, to different tasks within a construction project.

Resource Availability: The assessment of the availability and capacity of resources required for a construction project, including personnel, equipment, and materials.

Resource Breakdown Structure: A hierarchical breakdown of resources required for a construction project, often organized by category or type.

Resource Calendar: A schedule that outlines the availability and allocation of resources throughout a construction project.

Resource Leveling: The adjustment of resource allocation to ensure a balanced and efficient workflow throughout a construction project.

Retainage: The portion of a contract payment withheld until the completion of a construction project, usually done to ensure the contractor's performance.

R.F.I. (Request for Information): A formal inquiry by a contractor, subcontractor, or other project team member seeking clarification, additional details, or information about the project plans, specifications, or other relevant documents.

Ridge Beam: A horizontal beam at the roof's peak, supporting the rafters' upper ends.

Risk Management: The systematic process of identifying, analyzing, and mitigating potential risks that could impact the success of a construction project.

Risk Mitigation: Actions and strategies implemented to reduce the impact or likelihood of identified risks in a construction project.

Risk Monitoring and Control: Ongoing observation and management of risks throughout the construction project life cycle, focusing on implementing control measures.

Risk Owner: The individual or entity responsible for overseeing and managing a specific risk in a construction project.

Roof Truss: A structural framework designed to bridge the space above a room and support the roof.

S

Sanitary Access Charges (SAC): Fees or charges associated with accessing or utilizing sanitary infrastructure and services.

Scaffolding: Temporary structure, typically made of metal tubes and wooden planks, used by workers during construction, maintenance, or repair of buildings.

Schedule of Values: A detailed breakdown in a construction contract that assigns a specific value to each work component. It serves as a basis for progress payments and financial tracking.

Scope of Work: A comprehensive document outlining a construction project's specific tasks, activities, and deliverables. It defines the project's boundaries and details what the contract includes.

Scrum: An agile project management framework emphasizing collaboration, adaptability, and iterative development in construction projects.

Slack Time: In project scheduling, slack time or float is the time a task can be delayed without affecting the overall project timeline. It provides flexibility in the schedule.

Soft Costs: Costs in a construction project that are not directly related to physical construction but are necessary for the project's overall success. This includes fees, permits, legal expenses, and other non-construction expenses.

Specifications: Detailed written descriptions in construction documents outlining the construction project's materials, standards, and workmanship requirements.

Sprint: In agile project management, a time-boxed iteration of work, often 2 to 4 weeks, where specific tasks are completed.

Stand-Up Meeting: A brief and focused daily meeting in construction projects, where team members provide updates on progress and discuss challenges.

Structural Systems: The framework or structural elements that support a building or structure. This includes beams, columns, foundations, and other load-bearing components.

Submittal: Submitting construction documents, including shop drawings, product data, and samples, to the architect or engineer for approval.

Shop Drawing: Detailed drawings, diagrams, or plans created by contractors, manufacturers, or suppliers to illustrate how specific components will be fabricated and installed.

Sub (subcontractor): An abbreviation commonly used in the construction industry to refer to a subcontractor, a company hired by the main contractor to perform specific tasks or provide specialized services.

Substantial Completion: The stage in a construction project where the work is sufficiently complete that the owner can occupy or use the building for its intended purpose. It does not mean all work is finished, but the project is usable.

Substructure: The underlying support structure of a building or bridge, typically consisting of foundations, piers, and other components below ground level.

Superintendent: A key on-site management role overseeing day-to-day construction activities and ensuring adherence to plans, schedules, and quality standards.

T

Tar Paper: A water-resistant paper or building material impregnated with tar used as a moisture barrier in roofing and construction.

TI (Tenant Improvements): Modifications or alterations made to commercial or residential spaces to meet a tenant's specific needs or requirements. These improvements are typically undertaken by the tenant or at the tenant's request.

Time-and-a-half: A compensation rate for labor that is one and a half times the regular hourly wage. It is often applied for overtime work or work performed on holidays.

Time and Materials (T&M): A contract pricing model where the client pays for construction services based on the time spent and materials used.

Trade Contractor: A subcontractor specializing in a specific trade or craft, such as plumbing, electrical work, or HVAC installation.

Transmittal: A formal document used to transmit or send information, documents, or drawings from one party to another, often within a construction project team.

Trowel: A flat-bladed hand tool for spreading and smoothing mortar, plaster, or other materials.

Truss: A structural framework of beams or bars arranged in triangular or other geometric patterns to support a roof or bridge.

Tie Rod: A tension rod used in construction to provide support and stability by tying together different structural elements.

U

U-value: A measure of a building element's overall heat transfer coefficient, indicating its thermal insulation properties.

Underlayment: A material, often a layer of felt or foam, placed under the finish flooring to provide additional support, insulation, or moisture resistance.

Uniform Building Code: A set of standardized building codes or regulations that provide guidelines for construction and ensure safety, health, and structural integrity in the built environment.

Unit Prices: Cost per unit of measurement (e.g., cost per square foot) used in construction contracts, allowing flexibility in pricing for varying quantities of work.

Uplift: The upward force exerted on a structure, typically by wind or other environmental factors.

Utility Box: A box or enclosure used to house and protect utility connections, such as electrical or plumbing components

V

Value Engineering: A systematic process of reviewing and analyzing a construction project to identify opportunities to achieve cost savings or improve performance without sacrificing quality.

Vapor Barrier: A material or layer designed to impede the movement of water vapor, often installed in walls, roofs, or floors to prevent condensation.

Vendor: A supplier or seller of construction projects' goods, materials, or equipment. Vendors provide the products needed for construction.

Veneer: A thin decorative layer of material applied to the surface of a wall, floor, or furniture to enhance its appearance.

Vent Pipe: A vertical pipe that facilitates the movement of air, gases, or odors from plumbing systems to the exterior of a building.

Vinyl Siding: Exterior cladding made of polyvinyl chloride (PVC) is designed to mimic the appearance of traditional wood siding, offering durability and low maintenance.

W

Warranty: A written guarantee provided by a contractor or manufacturer that assures the quality and performance of work or products for a specified period after completion.

Water Access Charges (WAC): Fees or charges associated with accessing and utilizing water supply and distribution services within a community or area.

Wainscoting: Decorative wooden paneling applied to the lower part of a wall, often used for aesthetic purposes or to protect the wall from damage.

Waterfall Model: A traditional project management approach where tasks are completed sequentially, flowing downward like a waterfall, with each phase dependent on the completion of the previous one.

Waterproofing: The application of materials or treatments to prevent water penetration, making structures resistant to water damage or leakage.

Weep Hole: Small openings in structures, such as retaining walls or masonry, are designed to allow water drainage and prevent water accumulation.

Work in Progress (WIP): Construction tasks that are ongoing but not yet completed.

Work in Progress Limit: The maximum amount of ongoing construction work that a team or project can handle effectively.

Work Order: A formal document issued by the project owner or contractor instructing a contractor or subcontractor to proceed with a specific scope of work, often detailing requirements and terms.

Work scope: A detailed description of the work in a construction project, outlining tasks, responsibilities, and deliverables.

X

X-bracing: Diagonal bracing in the form of an "X" is used to provide stability to structural components, commonly employed in the design of buildings and frameworks.

Xeriscaping: Landscaping and gardening practices that reduce or eliminate the need for supplemental water, emphasizing water-efficient and drought-resistant plants

Xylene: A solvent commonly used in construction and industry for tasks such as paint thinning, cleaning, and adhesion promotion.

X-ray Diffraction (XRD): A technique used in construction materials analysis to determine the crystallographic structure of substances by analyzing how X-rays interact with them

Y

Yield Strength: The stress a material can endure without permanent deformation or failure, a crucial property in structural and material engineering.

Yoke: A horizontal bar or piece that connects and supports other structural elements, often used in various construction applications.

Yttrium: A chemical element often used in construction materials, alloys, and certain technologies due to its unique properties

Z

Z-bar: A metal bar shaped like the letter "Z," commonly used in construction for structural support or as a framing component.

Zoning: The division of land into different zones or areas with specific regulations governing land use, building types, and development.

Zigzag Joint: A joint or connection where components are joined in a zigzag pattern, often used for aesthetic purposes or to enhance structural integrity.

CONCLUSION

As we wrap up our deep dive into construction project management, let's take a moment to think about what we've learned. We've covered so much information, from the basics to real-life examples to looking at the future of construction with new technologies. It's probably safe to say you now have a pretty good understanding of how construction managers play a significant role in building things that develop our communities.

Starting with the basics, we outlined the essential parts of construction management, like setting the stage for a construction project and understanding different aspects like planning and finances. Then, we looked at real-world situations in residential, commercial, and industrial construction. We identified challenges in different job site scenarios and learned some valuable lessons. These stories showed us how vital good construction management is as we build and create structures that impact people's lives.

Looking ahead, we explored new technologies changing the game in construction management. From essential tools like Building Information Modeling and drones to 3D printing and augmented reality, these technologies bring construction into the technological realm, making things more efficient, cost-effective, and beneficial to the major stakeholders of construction projects.

As construction evolves toward the future, we see construction management continuing to grow with new technologies, a better understanding of how construction impacts the environment, and following global trends to provide the smallest carbon footprint imaginable on construction projects. It's not just about building things; it's about making spaces that last and are built to withstand decades of weather. I can see a future where construction managers aren't just people who provide the logistics on construction projects but are also innovation leaders, caring for the environment and positively impacting society.

For you as a future construction manager reading this, here's a simple thought to carry with you: Embrace the world of construction management. Construction is an exciting industry and will continue to be a valuable industry for centuries to come. Keep seeking knowledge, aim to do great work, and always strive to make a positive difference. Remember, every building you work on isn't just a bunch of blueprints and materials; it's a testament to your skills and dedication.

As we close this book, remember that the world's infrastructure has a limited lifespan. There will be new things to learn and fresh ideas to try, and most importantly - new construction work will always be there. This means construction project management is not a fading occupation or a career choice that can be outsourced; it takes real people to build real buildings, which will never change.

So, keep learning and refining your construction management skills, and embrace the technology of the future that defines construction projects. Just as buildings are razed and rebuilt again or refreshed from top to bottom, the work always continues in the construction management world. Congratulations on becoming a construction project manager; you won't regret it!

ABOUT THE AUTHOR

Paul Mason lives in the upper Midwest region of the United States with his wife and his trusted writing companion, a knee-high pit bull terrier mix named Sugar. Paul is an independent author writing for SugarDog Publishing and has written multiple fiction and non-fiction books on various topics and fictional storylines that resonate with his readers.

CONTACT ME

(I PERSONALLY RESPOND TO EVERYONE
THAT CONTACTS ME!)

Hello to my readers!

I sincerely appreciate your support by reading this book and I always encourage my readers to contact me with questions or comments about the book you've just read.

If you have constructive crtiticism about anything I've written….let me know!

If you'd like more information about anything I've discussed in this book….Let me know!

If you'd like to share a story with me about how this book resonated with you…Let me know!

My direct email address is: pdmason@sugardogpublishing.com

ALSO BY P.D. MASON

Financially Smart Career Planning For Teens: The Roadmap to Making Informed Decisions In An Uncertain Job Market, Prevent Feeling Overwhelmed & Analysis Paralysis To Achieve Affordable College Degrees(2023, SugarDog Publishing)

Apprenticeship Career Planning for Teens: A Comprehensive Guide to Securing Apprenticeships in High Demand Industries Without Taking on Years of College Debt (2023, SugarDog Publishing)

Skilled Trade Career Planning For Teens: The Handbook of Lucrative Skilled Trades & High Paying Occupations That Don't Require Expensive College Degrees (2023, SugarDog Publishing)

Hands-On Career Planning For Teens: Success Without Student Loans (The Complete Three Book Series) (2023, SugarDog Publishing)

Travel Japan: Unveiling Culture, Language & Local Gems (2023, SugarDog Publishing)

8 Simple Techniques For Easy Kitchen Knife Sharpening: Keep Your Home Kitchen Knives Sharp Using Trusted Tools, Methods & Techniques Taught By Professionals! (2023, SugarDog Publishing)

REFERENCES

Works Cited

"4 Steps for Handling Unexpected Conditions Claims on Construction Projects." *Www.mcdonaldhopkins.com*, 19 July 2018, www.mcdonaldhopkins.com/insights/news/Four-steps-for-handling-unexpected-conditions-clai.

"5 Key Components of Effective Leadership in Construction Project Management." *Bridgit*, 8 June 2021, gobridgit.com/blog/5-key-components-of-effective-leadership-in-construction-project-management/.

"5 Key Components of Effective Leadership in Construction Project Management." *Bridgit*, 8 June 2021, gobridgit.com/blog/5-key-components-of-effective-leadership-in-construction-project-management/.

"10 Ways to Improve Cash Flow in Construction." *Investopedia*, 2019, www.investopedia.com/articles/professionals/061215/10-ways-improve-cash-flow-construction.asp.

"A Guide to Construction Contract Management." *Parley pro | Contract Management Software Built for Today*, 19 Oct. 2022, parleypro.com/blog/construction-contract-management-a-to-z-guide/. Accessed 16 Oct. 2023.

Andony, Brock. "Construction Risk Management: The Comprehensive Guide." *MyComply*, 14 July 2022, mycomply.net/info/blog/construction-risk-management/.

---. "Construction Risk Management: The Comprehensive Guide." *MyComply*, 14 July 2022, mycomply.net/info/blog/construction-risk-management/.

buildern. "Most Common Construction Management Challenges and Why They Occur." *Buildern Resources*, 8 Feb. 2022, buildern.com/resources/blog/most-common-construction-management-challenges-and-why-they-occur/.

"Building Systems: An Introduction." *Pages.uoregon.edu*, pages.uoregon.edu/ftepfer/SchlFacilities/BuildingSystIntro.html.

Catalog of Construction Case Studies. 2022.

"Construction Industry - Compliance | Occupational Safety and Health Administration." *Www.osha.gov*, www.osha.gov/construction/compliance.

"Construction Industry | Occupational Safety and Health Administration." *Www.osha.gov*, www.osha.gov/construction.

"Construction Managers : Occupational Outlook Handbook: : U.S. Bureau of Labor Statistics." *Bls.gov*, 13 July 2018, www.bls.gov/ooh/management/construction-managers.htm.

"Construction Managers : Occupational Outlook Handbook: : U.S. Bureau of Labor Statistics." *Www.bls.gov*, www.bls.gov/ooh/management/construction-managers.htm#:~:text=Construction%20managers%2C%20often%20-called%20general. Accessed 16 Oct. 2023.

"Construction Risk Management: 5 Steps to Reduce & Mitigate Risk." *Procore,* www.procore.com/library/construction-risk-management.

"Contingency Planning in Construction Projects." *Construction Lawyer & Building Solicitors Sydney | Contracts Specialist Law Firm,* 9 Apr. 2023, www.contractsspecialist.com.au/articles/importance-contingency-planning-construction-projects/.

Dashore, Akshay. "Methods of Cost Estimation in Projects - Tools and Techniques." *The Constructor,* 16 Jan. 2019, theconstructor.org/construction/methods-cost-estimation/36532/.

---. "Methods of Cost Estimation in Projects - Tools and Techniques." *The Constructor,* 16 Jan. 2019, theconstructor.org/construction/methods-cost-estimation/36532/.

"Fundamentals of Scheduling & Resource Leveling." *Pmi.org,* 2019, www.pmi.org/learning/library/scheduling-resource-leveling-project-progression-8006.

Gabrieyel, Julie . "5 Essential Phases of Construction Project Management." *Jonas Construction Software,* 8 Apr. 2021, www.jonasconstruction.com/blog/phases-of-construction-project-management/.

HeadLight. "5 Major Challenges Facing the Infrastructure Construction Industry Today." *HeadLight,* 3 Nov. 2022, www.headlight.com/blog/daily-construction-reports/5-major-challenges-facing-the-infrastructure-construction-industry-today/. Accessed 16 Oct. 2023.

"How to Use a Gantt Chart for Project Management." *Wrike.com,* 2019, www.wrike.com/project-management-guide/faq/how-to-use-a-gantt-chart-for-project-management/.

"Importance of Communication in the Construction Industry (11 Reasons)." *Www.sablono.com,* www.sablono.com/en/blog/importance-of-communication-in-the-construction-industry.

Industrial Construction Case Studies | O3 Solutions. o3.solutions/why-o3/case-studies/. Accessed 16 Oct. 2023.

Killough, Dawn. "Construction Risk Management: 5 Steps to Reduce & Mitigate Risk." *Procore,* 23 Aug. 2023, www.procore.com/library/construction-risk-management.

Kolade, Anuoluwapo. "Fundamentals of Structural Design: Key Principles and Concepts." *C-E Channel,* 13 June 2023, koladeanu.wordpress.com/2023/06/13/fundamentals-of-structural-design-key-principles-and-concepts/. Accessed 16 Oct. 2023.

OpticVyu. "Top 10 Construction Project Management Challenges and Issues." *OpticVyu,* 25 Mar. 2021, blog.opticvyu.com/construction-project-management-challenges/.

Page, Michael. "Top 6 Construction Project Challenges | Michael Page US." *Michael Page,* 2019, www.michaelpage.com/advice/management-advice/top-6-construction-project-challenges.

"PMI Case Study Library." *Pmi.org,* 2019, www.pmi.org/business-solutions/case-studies.

Ramos, Diana. "Critical Path Method for Construction | Smartsheet." *Smartsheet,* 2019, www.smartsheet.com/construction-critical-path.

"Seven Construction Associations You Should Consider Joining." *Www.fieldwire.com,* www.fieldwire.com/blog/construction-associations-you-should-consider-joining/. Accessed 16 Oct. 2023.

"StackPath." *Www.forconstructionpros.com*, www.forconstructionpros.com/business/business-services/training-education/article/21563426/bridgit-6-best-certifications-for-construction-career-development.

Stannard, Liam. "17 Construction Technology Advancements to Watch in 2020 | BigRentz." *Https://Www.bigrentz.com*, 2 Feb. 2020, www.bigrentz.com/blog/construction-technology.

Taylor, DP. "Construction Management: Understanding Cost Control." *The Motley Fool*, 18 May 2022, www.fool.com/the-ascent/small-business/construction-management/articles/cost-control-in-construction/.

The Constructor. "Risk Management in Construction Projects." *The Constructor*, 20 Sept. 2018, theconstructor.org/construction/risk-management-construction-projects/24873/.

"The Role of Government Regulations in Construction Safety." *Kcal's Architecture Insights*, 24 Feb. 2023, www.architecturearea.com/entry/The-Role-of-Government-Regulations-in-Construction-Safety. Accessed 16 Oct. 2023.

todd. "Construction Project Team Structure: Roles and Responsibilities." *Tool Tracking Software*, 20 June 2022, gocodes.com/construction-project-team-structure/.

"Top 90 Construction Management Firms for 2022." *Building Design + Construction*, 22 Aug. 2022, www.bdcnetwork.com/top-90-construction-management-firms-2022.

United States Department of Labor. "Law and Regulations | Occupational Safety and Health Administration." *Osha.gov*, 2016, www.osha.gov/laws-regs.

Wood, Fasken-Deanne, et al. "The Importance of Insurance in Construction Projects | Lexology." *Www.lexology.com*, www.lexology.com/library/detail.aspx?g=ac899909-5dcf-4c03-909b-95e9794653e5.

www.researchgate.net/publication/216639054_Time_Cost_and_Quality_Trade-off_Analysis_in_Construction_of_Projects.

Epa.gov, 17 July 2003, archive.epa.gov/greenbuilding/web/html/whybuild.html.

www.ingramcontent.com/pod-product-compliance
Lightning Source LLC
Chambersburg PA
CBHW070523160726
48003CB00004B/1673